PREGNANCY made comfortable with Yoga and Dietetics

A complete reference book covering all stages from pre-pregnancy to post-pregnancy

Nishtha Saraswat

V&S PUBLISHERS

AF674606

Published by:

V&S PUBLISHERS

F-2/16, Ansari road, Daryaganj, New Delhi-110002
☎ 23240026, 23240027 • *Fax:* 011-23240028
info@vspublishers.com • www.vspublishers.com

Online Brandstore: amazon.in/vspublishers

Regional Office : Hyderabad
5-1-707/1, Brij Bhawan (Beside Central Bank of India Lane)
Bank Street, Koti, Hyderabad - 500 095
☎ 040-24737290
vspublishershyd@gmail.com

Follow us on:

BUY OUR BOOKS FROM: AMAZON FLIPKART

© **Copyright:** V&S PUBLISHERS

ISBN 978-93-813849-2-3
New Edition

DISCLAIMER

While every attempt has been made to provide accurate and timely information in this book, neither the author nor the publisher assumes any responsibility for errors, unintended omissions or commissions detected therein. The author and publisher makes no representation or warranty with respect to the comprehensiveness or completeness of the contents provided.
All matters included have been simplified under professional guidance for general information only, without any warranty for applicability on an individual. Any mention of an organization or a website in the book, by way of citation or as a source of additional information, doesn't imply the endorsement of the content either by the author or the publisher. It is possible that websites cited may have changed or removed between the time of editing and publishing the book.
Results from using the expert opinion in this book will be totally dependent on individual circumstances and factors beyond the control of the author and the publisher.
It makes sense to elicit advice from well informed sources before implementing the ideas given in the book. The reader assumes full responsibility for the consequences arising out from reading this book.
For proper guidance, it is advisable to read the book under the watchful eyes of parents/guardian. The buyer of this book assumes all responsibility for the use of given materials and information.
The copyright of the entire content of this book rests with the author/publisher. Any infringement/transmission of the cover design, text or illustrations, in any form, by any means, by any entity will invite legal action and be responsible for consequences thereon.

Printed at : Param Offsetters, Okhla, New Delhi–110020

DEDICATED TO

My mother Isht Sharma

&

My father, Guru and inspiration

'Padma Shri' Bharat Bhushan

who have dedicated their lives to the

benefit of mankind

Acknowledgements

While writing this book I realised that we cannot accomplish anything alone in this world. Having the idea of the content, the willingness to trudge along the path and putting in all you have is only half the job done. The other half is accomplished when you get the requisite ingredients in the form of encouragement, love and empathy from the ones who love you and who care for you. I would like to thank my husband Neeraj Saraswat, who helped me in giving a definite shape to my thoughts, for his guidance, encouragement, patience (when I worked for hours continuously on this project), and the confidence he showed in me. Otherwise, it was difficult to accomplish this project for a working housewife.

My sincere thanks to my beloved sister Pratishtha Sharma (Yoga Consultant 'Amatra' Spa, Hotel Ashoka, New Delhi) and demonstrators-cum-friends Dr Jitendra Saini (M.Sc., P.D. Yoga) who is a yoga teacher at Indian High Commission, Mauritius and Mrs. Seema Sharma, for giving their precious time for the photo sessions.

My special thanks to Mr. R.A. Gupta, who appreciated my thought process, showed confidence in my writing and guided me well all along.

And last but certainly not the least, my sincere gratitude to all my family members who stood by me and encouraged me all through the writing of this book.

Contents

Section 4: Understanding Pregnancy

Section 5: The First Trimester

Section 6: The Second Trimester

Section 7: The Third Trimester

Section 8: Post-Pregnancy

Appendix

Preface

There are few happier moments in a woman's life than successfully giving birth to a kicking and healthy baby. Attaining motherhood transforms a woman forever and extracts out a persona lying dormant for years deep within her. Preparing for pregnancy and living through those fantastic nine months, moment by moment, is an experience that a woman can never forget in her lifetime.

Pregnancy, the stage of conceiving another life within, leading to the birth of the baby .can be broadly classified into three periods — pre, during and post pregnancy. Each period has its own significance, characteristics and complications. Various phases during pregnancy bring about a lot of changes in a woman's life at all levels, physical, mental, emotional and social.

This book is an effort in the direction of understanding the process of pregnancy from all possible dimensions and providing an insight to the reader or should I say the user, which should help her in making the whole process of pregnancy more enjoyable and problem-free. The means to an easy, enjoyable and problem-free pregnancy has been provided through an amalgamation of the regular practice of the ancient Indian science of yoga and the modern yet relevant subject of 'Dietetics'. I can say this as I have been practising yoga since a tender age of three years under the guidance of my father, Yoga Guru '*Padma Shri*' Bharat Bhushan and have seen innumerable cases of pregnant women who have been benefited from the application of various modules of yoga and correct diet.

Readers can use this book as a reference during various stages of pregnancy and can find solutions to most of the problems that occur at all those stages. Amazingly, most of the problems associated with pregnancy can be cured with simple application of 'Yoga and Diet'. A proactive and regular application of the suggested yogic techniques and correct diet plan will help them enjoy their pregnancy in a wholesome manner. Pictures, illustrations and charts have been used in the book extensively to make it user-friendly, practical and easy to understand.

The contents of the book are an outcome of my personal experience in the field of yoga as a demonstrator in my earlier years with my father and as an exponent and consultant later. Being a student and then a professor of the extremely relevant subject of Health and Nutrition has given me direction and courage to combine the benefits of Yoga and dietetics and present them to the reader for best usage. The contents have been further substantiated and augmented with information from various textbooks, journals and articles published in India and abroad in various media.

The effort has been to keep the book as simple and usable as possible. The best way to use the book is to live with it during all phases of pregnancy, even though various sections of the book are complete unto themselves. Even those who are planning for their pregnancy can benefit as the book begins with pre-pregnancy stage.

— Nishtha Saraswat

Foreword

It is indeed a pleasant experience to write about this book by Nishtha Saraswat whom I witnessed from early childhood performing yoga on national and international platforms and growing into a well-shaped Yog-Sadhika. She earned depth of yoga in *sanskaras* inherited from her father, world renowned Yoga Guru Shri Bharat Bhushan, the founder of Mokshayatan International Yogashram at Saharanpur and first ever *'Padma Shri'* awardee by the President of India for his excellence and contribution to enrich the great Indian heritage of science of yoga. Nishtha succeeded in giving a scientific vision and reason to yoga during her studies of M.Sc. and she could see and suggest the practice of yoga suiting to particular requirements of the individuals.

Under modern lifestyle of comforts, maternity is growing tough and complicated day by day as women in modern society leave all exercises and even normal physical activities as soon as pregnancy is confirmed. Even newly wedded women are bound to face the consequences of such comforts in the form of frequent complications and caesarean deliveries. As a result, they lose right of healthy life just after one or two deliveries and pregnancy becomes a threat to their life instead of joy of motherhood. Scientific observations now claim that exercises even during pregnancy do not disturb the motherhood but on the contrary help enjoying joy of health, easy pregnancy and balanced growth of baby in the womb followed by comfortable delivery. Readers will learn from this book that yoga is not merely a set of physical exercises but a lifestyle to heal and highlight the spirits of women even under challenging circumstances and the best way to help the baby grow physically, mentally, emotionally and even spiritually. Pregnancy is the time when a baby taking shape in the womb is directly governed by the physical, mental and emotional state of the mother. Indian *rishis* noticed the significance of this special period and made it a part of *Sanskar Vidhi* to guide us for pre, during and post-pregnancy preparations to grow a holy being who is going to descend on this earth in the form of a baby.

I have gone through the book and I feel that this book will fulfil the requirement not only of a pregnant lady under special circumstances but of newly shaping baby and the society at large. The author seems to have observed the gradual changes in women and the baby during pregnancy and has suggested special yoga programme most favourable to enjoy pregnancy with dos and don'ts and the diet discipline to bring perfect results of yoga practice during this period. I feel that this book will prove to be the best friend to a woman to help her during pregnancy and will become the need of every family as motherhood is the foundation stone of the family. My best wishes to this noble effort of the author and the publisher.

Vasant Panchmi. Vikram Samvat 2063

Dated: January 23, 2007

Ishwar Bhardwaj
Professor & Head
Department of Human Consciousness & Yogic Sciences
Gurukul Kangri Vishwavidyalaya, Haridwar

Pregnancy, Yoga and Dietetics

The word 'Pregnancy' brings with itself a variety of emotions. On one hand, it means devoting the conjugal life towards divine process of '*Srijan*' or creation, expectations of a new life descending on earth, unbridled joy, happiness, excitement and expansion. On the other hand, it also means the beginning of a long wait, anxiety, pain and labour. Whatever it may mean to different people, a common aspect of pregnancy is a couple's involvement in creation with a series of possible complications associated with it. Though being pregnant and ultimately being able to give birth to a life is a wonderful, enriching and fulfilling experience and a pride for a woman, but it can also be a difficult and even harrowing experience with lasting impact on both the mother and the child. This, therefore, becomes extremely important that pregnancy be handled in such a manner that not only the outcome but the process of pregnancy itself becomes easy, enjoyable and pleasant. What to say of mother, even the baby in the womb should not pass through any unpleasant experience of screaming with fear or blowing with rage as it will always result in an unbalanced development of the baby.

The question arises as to why should pregnancy be treated any differently from the normal period in one's life? The answer to this lies behind the simple fact that pregnancy is different from other phases in one's life as it involves carrying two lives in one body, which never happens during any other phase of life. And the new life which is carried totally depends on the carrier for everything it needs for its further existence till it comes out into the world to be identified as independent entity. Giving birth to a healthy baby is so important a task that Indian *rishis* prescribed special *Sanskars* as *Garbhadhan Sanskar, Punsavan Sanskar* and *Jaatkarm Sanskar* to give proper guidelines to the couple to perform their duty towards humanity in a perfect way and develop the child properly. In other words, all phases involved in pregnancy must be given due attention and care.

The various phases involved in pregnancy are:

1. Pre-pregnancy, where one gets physically, mentally and emotionally ready to sow the seed of life
2. Conception or beginning of pregnancy, wherein the fertilisation happens and the seed of life is sown
3. First trimester or the first three months of the pregnancy, during which the life inside the mother takes shape
4. Second trimester or the next three months of the development of life inside the mother's womb
5. Third trimester or the last three months of pregnancy, which culminate in the delivery and birth of the baby
6. The critical post-pregnancy period, which is as important as the pregnancy itself

Every phase during pregnancy has its own significance in terms of the impact that it has on the lives of the mother and the child. Any one phase not handled well can have long term repercussions and can be detrimental in various ways for the mother and the newly born. Each phase should thus be first understood thoroughly for its significance and should be treated accordingly in order to make pregnancy enjoyable and a truly memorable experience.

What we need to know first about pregnancy and its various stages is the type and nature of the complications involved. Then we should also know how we can overcome those complications and can even avoid them. The dos and don'ts to be observed must be clear in our minds and the solution to most common problems at hand.

So, what is it that one can actually do to look forward to making pregnancy an enjoyable, pleasant and a memorable experience? Where can one find the answers to the most common problems and complications that occur during pregnancy? Is there something that is easy to understand and apply during those crucial nine months to make pregnancy problem-free? Is there something that can be cent percent effective with no side-effects? What should an expectant and expecting mother look up to during that period?

The answer to these important and relevant questions lies within the realms of the two of the most relevant social subjects of modern times, the ancient Indian scientific art of 'Yoga' and the most significant arm of the subject of Health and Nutrition Sciences 'Dietetics'.

Yoga

Yoga has become one of the most spoken and commonly heard word in the recent times. The word 'yoga' is derived from the Sanskrit meaning of the word, which means 'to join' and can be understood as meaning 'Unity' or 'Oneness'. Yoga is not, as many would believe, an ancient art that has mythological heritage, nor is it, as the popular belief goes, only about '*Asanas*' and '*Pranayamas*'. Yoga, in its true essence, is the science of living in the right manner. It ensures 'the right living' during all stages of life viz. 'Infancy', 'Childhood', Adolescence', 'Adulthood', 'Middle Age' and even 'Ripe Old Age'. It encompasses all aspects of the personality — 'Physical', 'Mental', 'Vital', 'Emotional', 'Psychic' and 'Spiritual'. This is achieved through various forms of yoga.

Yoga creates an environment of dynamic peacefulness and harmony within. On a physical level, it strengthens and tones various parts of the body and improves flexibility, stamina and mobility. Biologically it does a balancing act on different systems of the body, helps increase vitality, strengthens immunity, detoxifies the body and improves all biological processes and brain functioning. Mentally, it increases sensory awareness, improves concentration levels, clears the thought process and relaxes the mind, focuses attention and frees the spirit. And most importantly, it keeps away negativity on all three levels.

The eight forms of a comprehensive yogic system (*Ashtanga Yoga*) according to Sage Patanjali include:

- *Yama* – moral duties such as *Ahimsa* (non-violence), *Satya* (truth), *Brahmacharya* (celibacy), *Aparigraha* (self-restraint)
- *Niyama* – self-observances such as purification of inner self through discipline, *Shoucha* (inner cleansing), *Santosha* (contentment), *Swadhyay* (self-introspection), *Ishwar Pranidhan* (devotion to Almighty)
- *Asana* – physical yogic exercises
- *Pranayama* – breathing techniques
- *Pratyahara* – dissociation of self-consciousness from outer world
- *Dharana* – concentration on a particular subject
- *Dhyana* – meditation
- *Samadhi* – identification with pure consciousness, self-actualisation

Self-actualisation or identification with the pure consciousness is the pinnacle of achievement and ultimate aim of being a *yogi* (one who observes and practises all aspects of yoga in daily life).

What makes yoga so powerful a medium is the fact that it takes the holistic route of unification and harmony. Yoga provides individuals with their own way to connecting with their true selves. Such is the flexibility and adaptability of yoga that it transcends all barriers of place, religion, faith, caste, and creed and establishes connection with everyone who wants to embrace it for well-being.

The science of yoga can be safely and effectively applied during all stages of life for enlightened and problem-free living and pregnancy is no exception to this. Yoga, if practised regularly under restraint and guidance, is known to have an immensely positive impact during all phases of pregnancy. The process of pregnancy will never be the same again if yogic techniques are applied and practised correctly. The entire experience of pregnancy will then be as pleasant as the outcome itself.

The most significant advantage of making yoga a daily ingredient of one's life during pregnancy is that if followed correctly there are only positive effects that are seen. Unlike any other mode of modern treatment or medication, there are no harmful side-effects of practising yoga in the right manner.

Benefits of Yoga during Pregnancy

- Yoga minimises the discomforts and complications faced during different stages of pregnancy. Yoga improves the circulation of blood, which really helps in dealing with different functional changes occurring in the body.

- Yoga stretches the body, and therefore makes it flexible to deal with the increasing weight. It also helps in maintaining the balance between body weight and body mass index.
- Yoga uses breathing exercises called pranayama to calm the body and the mind by proper functioning of endocrine system of the body.

Benefits of Yoga during Child Delivery

- Yoga ensures a comfortable and easy delivery. With regular practice of yoga throughout the pregnancy, the body parts which play an active role during the process of delivery become flexible, toned and strong. Many women who practise yoga regularly have found delivery to be much easier.
- Yoga stretches all ligaments throughout the pelvic, hip, and leg area, resulting in easier positioning and pushing during labour.
- In the birth process, breathing plays an important role and is an important part of a successful delivery. Regular practice of pranayama keeps the pregnant ladies more in-synch with their breath, which prepares them well for power-breathing in different stages of labour pains.

Benefits of Yoga post-Pregnancy

- Yoga plays an important role in getting you back in shape post-delivery both externally and internally. It massages the internal organs gently which have gone through a lot of stress in past nine months and re-tones them. Yoga helps in overcoming post-pregnancy discomforts and problems such as stretch marks, piles, excessive bleeding, loss of bladder control, insomnia etc.
- Yoga stretches and strengthens the body in all directions and areas. This helps to get the whole body back in shape quickly after pregnancy and delivery.

Dietetics

A branch of the vast yet recent subject of health and nutrition sciences, dietetics deals with the study of diets in health and disease. The relevance of nutrition in one's diet cannot be overemphasised as it is extremely important to receive continuous and optimum nutrition to remain healthy.

Dietetics in today's context assumes importance owing to the fact that a large number of newer food products, convenience and fast foods, fad diet foods etc are being introduced every day. The changing lifestyles and fast pace of life today leaves little time with individuals to be able to assess their nutritive and dietary needs and requirements. It becomes even more significant to introduce dietetics as a part of daily life as there is a need to be sensitive about nutrition, health, hygiene and sanitation aspects of the food. More so when most of the available food products are made to suit the palate rather than keep the above mentioned aspects of nutrition in mind.

The use of diets in treatment and prevention of diseases and maintenance of health is referred to as Diet Therapy, Therapeutic nutrition or Dietotherapy. Diet therapy is generally used as a supplement to medical or surgical treatment. However, it will not be an exaggeration to state that in certain cases diet itself becomes the most important aspect in a patient's treatment. The immediate examples that come to mind are that of the treatment of diabetes mellitus, obesity, gastro-intestinal ailments etc.

Dietetics and diet therapy play an even greater role during various stages of pregnancy. The nutritional requirements undergo a great deal of change during various phases of pregnancy due to the additional burden of nourishing the foetus, which depends totally on the primary diet of the carrying woman for all its nutritional requirements.

A lot of problems and complications that occur during different phases of pregnancy can be prevented, treated or reduced with application of diet therapy. It is thus essential to include the recommended diet and dietary allowances to the women during pregnancy irrespective of their age, class, creed, education, occupation, socio-economic status and social or political placement.

Yoga and Dietetics in Pregnancy

When yoga as well as dietetics alone can do wonders in keeping an individual healthy and free from diseases, one cannot help but imagine the kind of impact that the combination of the two can make.

Yoga and dietetics are two of the most potent subjects that must be brought to the fore for the overall benefit of humanity. Both the disciplines actually complement each other and the benefits can become manifold if the synergy of yoga and dietetics is utilised in the correct manner.

Yoga is said to be incomplete without observing strict discipline in one's diet. Yoga advocates *Satvik* or simple and minimal diet that is largely vegetarian and full of nutrients, required specifically during any stage of life or while treating any abnormality. Out of the three ways of food intake, direct from sunlight (as in plants), from plants (as in herbivorous animals and vegetarian human beings) and from animals which eat plants (as in carnivores and non-vegetarian human beings), yoga considers fulfilling food requirements through consumption of plants and their products as the best. In the same manner, any diet can be doubly effective if yogic discipline is inculcated in one's daily routine.

This, therefore, is of prime importance that yoga and dietetics be combined and their synergistic benefits be used to treat most of the problems associated with pregnancy. The application of yoga and dietetics becomes important during pregnancy since the primary requirement during various phases of pregnancy include keeping the mother physically, mentally and emotionally fit and healthy able to endure the hardships of pregnancy. And at the same time, the nutritional requirements of both the mother-to-be and the foetus are to be met in order to maintain the woman's health and to encourage healthy development of the foetus.

Yoga and dietetics can be safely applied and embraced during pregnancy as neither has negative side-effects and still can be used to sort out most of the common problems associated with pregnancy without medication or surgery.

Researches have proved that regular physical activity coupled with the right nutritional intake and the right frame of mind helps in bearing with the demands of pregnancy and ultimately results in normal delivery of a healthy baby with no or minimal after effects. And the fact that there is no better alternative to yoga and dietetics to fulfil these criteria, points to the inherent need of applying the two for a wonderful experience during all stages of pregnancy.

> "*Yoga had always intrigued me and I wanted to experience it myself. I came to India and during one such yoga camp, met Nishtha. It was then that I came to know about benefits of yoga during pregnancy. I learnt everything that was needed to have a 'yogic' pregnancy in a month's time. I went back and applied whatever I had learnt when I and my husband planned our family. Right from conceiving to delivering a smiling pink baby, I enjoyed my pregnancy thoroughly. Ask me and I would recommend everyone to practise yoga and the specific diet plan during your pregnancy.*"
>
> — Sarah Smith, Illinois, USA

Pre-Pregnancy

Making up Your Mind

The social landscape is undergoing a transformational change today. Both men and women have begun to share equal responsibilities in almost every aspect of their lives. Almost all decisions are being taken with mutual consent. Most important among them is to become parents, because parenting, though most beautiful, is also the most challenging responsibility to share. It demands time, patience, resources and most importantly the mutual understanding between husband and wife. Always remember that only a happy couple can give birth to a happy child. Giving birth is not just an overnight job. It is a pleasure, pride and duty to be performed religiously by mother with active and dedicated cooperation of the father.

'Sanskar Vidhi' introduced by Vedic rishis and yogis enables the parents to give birth to an all round perfect baby called santaan. It is called santaan only because its root is at sanskar. Garbhadhaan Sanskar, determines the proper time, process, precautions and diet before and after Garbhadhaan for gaining a pious and perfectly built generation, and for maintaining sound health of the parents.

Getting Ready

Once a positive decision on parenthood has been taken, a couple needs to give itself three to four months' time to prepare itself mentally, emotionally and physically. It is not only the woman who has to prepare herself for the motherhood but the man also has to share equal burden on his way to fatherhood and therefore needs adequate preparation.

Getting Ready Mentally

A strong mindset during pregnancy paves the way for an easy and enjoyable gestation period. It is extremely important for the future parents to become mentally prepared for a transformation in their lifestyle. However, it is essential for a couple to change the habits, which may become impediment in their path to parenthood. Some of the most common habits that need to be changed the day a couple decides to become parents are:

- **Say goodbye to stress:** Stress is the biggest factor responsible for the decreased levels of testosterone and sperm count. If stress is bothering you then get rid of it. Include meditation and yoga in your daily routine and adopt a positive attitude towards everything. This will help enhance potency.

- **Quit smoking and alcohol:** Smoking and alcohol reduce the chances of pregnancy drastically and affect both partners. These are two of the most important factors to get rid of, while preparing for pregnancy. A strong mental makeup is required to quit these evil habits. Quitting them optimises the chances of conceiving. With the practice of yoga and meditation, it is easy to get rid of these habits.

Getting Ready Emotionally

Getting ready emotionally is very important because pregnancy is a period of outflow of emotions. It is a period to be enjoyed together. Gaining emotional maturity during pregnancy helps the couple understand each other better and creates a stronger bond between them.

Develop compatibility and emotional bonding with your partner and create a happy atmosphere around you. Researches have proved that emotional bonding between the partners at the time of lovemaking boosts the chances of conceiving.

Getting Ready Physically

- **Check on your weight:** Have a close check on your weight. Find out whether you are overweight or underweight. Reaching closer to your ideal weight will help you cope better during pregnancy. Yoga and dietary control will help immensely in this regard.
- **Visit your doctor:** Visit your doctor and tell her about your decision. Go for medical checkups especially HIV test, blood test, sugar test and blood pressure test. You can also go for a follicle study with the consultation of your doctor, this will help you in determining your fertility period and the day the egg is released from the ovary. Do not forget to discuss the history of family illnesses like diabetes, heart problems etc, if any.
- **Wear easy clothes:** Synthetic and tight-fitted clothes can overheat a man's testicles and inhibit sperm production. One should avoid taking sauna baths, weight training in the gym, tough sports and activities that can cause injury to reproductive organs.
- **Check on medication:** If you are taking any medication then have a check on it as it may cause fertility problems. Ask your physician about the safety aspects of the medicines you may be taking.

Yoga before Pregnancy

Regular practice of yoga is an excellent pre-pregnancy makeup. It controls and enhances all the three abilities, physical, mental and emotional that determines beginning, course and outcome of pregnancy. In case one has never practised yoga earlier, there is a need to prepare in the right manner before getting in the groove.

Getting Started

- Ensure you are light at stomach. You may perform yoga empty stomach in early morning or before dinner in the evening.

- Wear comfortable loose-fitted cotton dress, preferably saffron, maroon, yellow or white colour.
- Suspend all involvements and appointments for the half an hour and make up your mind that nothing is going to disturb you now. *Yog sadhna* will make you more competent and able to face and deal with prevailing situations still better.
- Concentrate on proper breath and join mental chanting of holy 'OM' the ultimate *mantra* of wellness in this birth and beyond.
- For result-oriented yoga, make up your mind to depend on pure vegetarian food. Choose your food carefully and remember that your stomach is neither a dustbin nor a graveyard.
- Learn the art of forgiving and thank God for all goodness you are blessed with.
- Never perform *yogabhyaas* in a hurry. You may practise a little if you feel more packed some day but never miss your *sadhna*. Such regularity will lead you to encouraging and early results.
- Add amla, tulsi and honey to your daily intake and prefer cow's milk in daily use.
- Use a four fold blanket, yoga mat or cotton *asana* for *yogabhyaas* and prefer sitting facing east in the morning and facing west in the evening during yoga workout.
- Women should not perform regular *yogabhyaas* during menstruation. There is a separate regime to be followed during menstruation.

Observance of these pre-conditions for starting regular practice of yoga ensures that one can derive maximum out of the bottomless ocean of benefits from yoga.

Following are the forms of yoga that can be performed by both men and women while they prepare for parenthood. These yogic exercises help tone up the entire body, specifically the reproductive organs. They increase blood flow to various parts of the body, tone up the glandular system and ultimately ready you for perfect parenthood.

Asanas

1. Tadasana

- Stand with feet together, body weight equally distributed on both legs, and fingers interlocked in front of your chest with palms towards the ground.
- Pull your arms forward while inhaling through nostrils turning your palms to front and then lifting overhead with palms facing the sky.
- Hold the inhaled position as long as you can with complete body stretched upwards.
- Feel your ankles, calves, knee joints, thighs, pelvis, buttocks, trunk, chest, shoulders and arms perfectly stretched and pulled upwards.
- Balance yourself on the toes.
- Lower the heels and bring the hands beside your thighs while exhaling gently and relax.

Tadasana

Repetitions: Repeat the above mentioned steps 5 to 10 times.

2. Surya Namaskar

Step 1
- Stand upright with your feet together in prayer pose. Your eyes will remain closed. Breathe normally.

Step 2
- While inhaling, raise and stretch both your arms above the head.
- Bend the head, arms and upper trunk backward.

Step 3
- Bend forward while exhaling until the fingers or palms of the hands touch the ground on either side of the feet.
- Try to touch the knees with forehead while keeping the knees straight.

Step-1

Step-2

Step-3

Step 4
- Place the palms flat on the floor beside the feet.
- While inhaling, stretch the left leg back as far as possible.
- At the same time, bend the right knee, keeping the right foot on the floor in the same position. Keep the arms straight.
- In the final position, the weight of the body should be supported on the hands, the right foot, left knee and toes of the left foot. The head should be tilted backward, and the back arched.

Step 5
- While exhaling take the right foot back beside the left foot simultaneously, raise the buttocks and lower the head between the arms, so that the back and the legs form two sides of a triangle.
- Legs and arms should be straight in the final position.

- Try to keep the heels on the floor and bring the head towards the knees.

Step-4

Step-5

Step 6

- Lower the knees, chest and forehead to the floor.
- Only the toes, knees, chest, hands and forehead should touch the floor simultaneously. If this is not possible, first lower the knees, then the chest and finally the chin.
- The buttocks, hips and abdomen should be raised.
- The breath is held outside in this pose. There is no respiration.

Step-6

Step 7

- Lower the buttocks and hips to the floor.
- Straighten the elbows, arch the back, and push the chest forward into the cobra pose.

- While inhaling bend the head back and direct the gaze upward to the eyebrow centre.
- The thighs and hips remain on the floor and the arms support the trunk. Unless the spine is very flexible the arms will remain slightly bent.

Step-7

Step 8
- This stage is the repeat of step 5.
- From step 7 assume step 5, while exhaling raise the buttocks and lower the heels to the floor.

Step 9
- This stage is same as step 4.
- Keep the palms flat on the floor.
- Bend the left leg and bring the left foot forward between the hands.
- Simultaneously, lower the right knee so that it touches the floor and push the pelvis forward.
- Tilt the head backward, and arch the back.
- Inhale while assuming the pose

Step 10
- This position is a repeat of step 3.
- While exhaling bring the right foot forward next to the left foot.
- Straighten both knees.
- Bring the forehead as close to the knees as possible without straining.

Step 11
- This stage is a repeat of step 2.

Step 12
- This is the final position and the same as the step 1.
- Bring the palms together in front of the chest as in prayer pose while exhaling.

Repetitions: This is one round. Start with 5 such rounds and with practice and stamina make it to 10 to 12 rounds.

3. Paschimottanasana

- Sit on your yoga mat with legs outstretched, feet together, hands folded in prayer and spine straight but relaxed.
- Inhale gently while lifting the arms over your head and bend forward slowly from the hips, sliding the hands down the legs and toes.
- Try to grasp the big toes with your fingers and thumbs. Hold the ankles or any part of legs within your reach if it is impossible.

Paschimottanasana

- Try to bend forward gently without any jerk or force applied.
- Hold the position for a few seconds according to your capacity with relaxed back and leg muscles to develop more flexibility.
- Keep the leg straight at knee and try to bend the elbows. Bring the trunk down towards legs and try to touch the knees with the forehead.
- Hold this position for as long as you find comfortable. Return to the starting position while inhaling and lifting your arms over your head.
- Resume the prayer pose and relax with your palms placed on the floor behind your back and spine perfectly at ease.

Repetitions: Beginners may practise 3 to 5 rounds.

Breathing: Inhale while lifting your arms upward and exhale gently while bending forward. Breathe slow and deep in final position or retain the breath out if holding for a short duration. Keep your awareness at relaxation of the back muscles or at the slow and rhythmic breathing practice. This asana is strictly prohibited for people suffering from slipped disc or sciatica.

4. Katichakrasana

Step 1

- Spread your yoga mat on the floor and lie down on your back with your feet together and palms resting on the floor beside your thighs.
- Lift your arms up while inhaling till they reach above your head.
- Close the palms together and clasp your fingers.
- Keep the body above your waistline to upper side and the legs to lower side. Keep your toes pulled towards yourself.
- Hold the breath in and twist the lower body to left side in such a way that your right heel and hip are lifted from the floor.

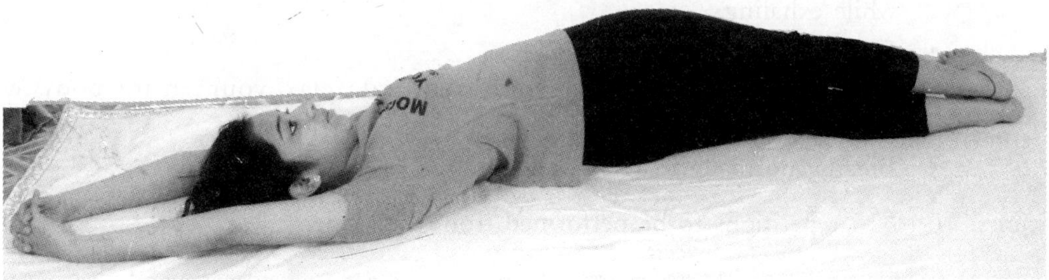

Step-1

- Hold your legs straight at knees and your upper body firm on the floor. Exhale as you move back to starting position. Repeat it on right side also.

Repetitions: This is one round. Repeat 10 to 15 such rounds.

Step 2

- Continue to lie on the floor.
- Fold your legs at knees and bring the heels close to the hips with arms resting under the head and elbows kept on the floor.
- Hold the knees and toes together so that both the soles are clearly visible.

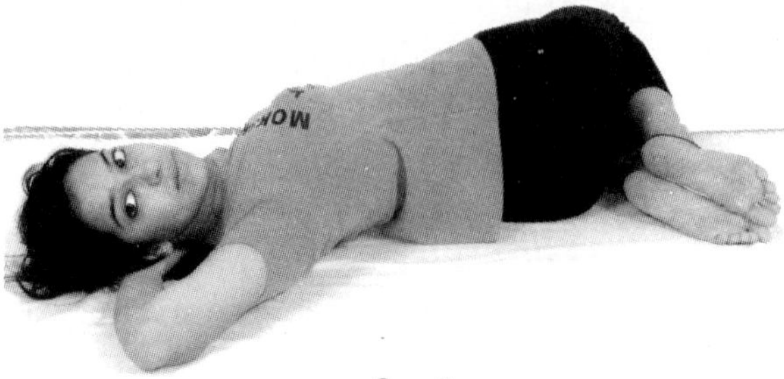

Step-2

- Maintain them together and inhale while moving the knees to left side and face to right side, but back and elbows will continue to remain firm on the floor.
- Come back to starting position while exhaling. Repeat the same on right side as well.

Repetitions: Repeat 10 to 15 times.

Step 3

- Continue to lie on the floor.
- Hold your left ankle with right hand and bring the left heel close between the thighs with sole firmly placed on the right thigh, left knee resting on the floor.
- Move the left knee to right side of the floor and face moving to left side at the same time. Remember to hold your left elbow on the floor while performing this act.
- Move your left knee and your face to their original positions, while exhaling.

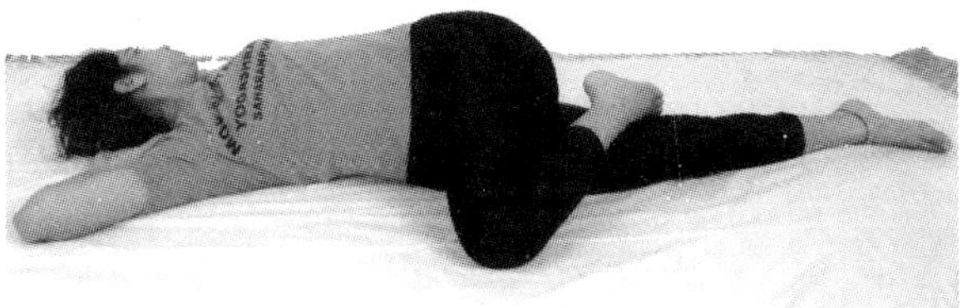

Step-3

- Follow the same process on left side also. Spread your legs and relax your entire body with all efforts withdrawn.
- Breathe normally to relax perfectly.

Repetitions: 10 to 15 repetitions to be performed from each side.

5. Pawanmuktasana

- Lie in the base position. Bend the right knee, grip it with both the hands, press the thigh against stomach and bring the knee closer to chest while exhaling.
- Keep the left leg straight on your mat.
- Bring the chin closer to your right knee. Continue breathing for better effect on stomach and the back and release all spinal tension.

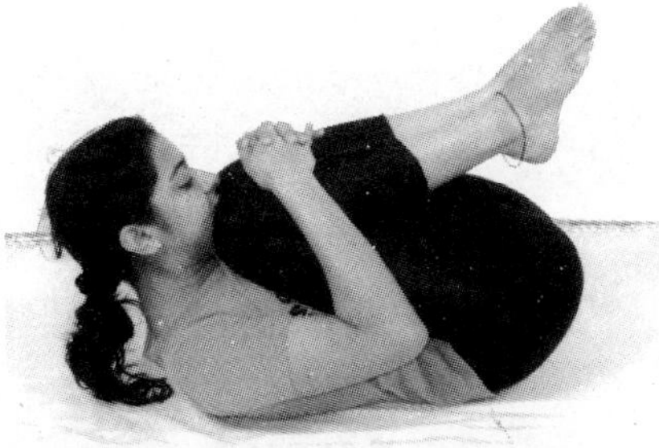

Pawanmuktasana

- Spread the right leg and return back to your original position while inhaling.
- Relax and breathe normally.
- Repeat the same on the left side and then on both the legs together. Always begin with right side and conclude on both together.

Repetitions: Repeat 3 to 5 times.

6. Uttanpadasana

- Lie down on your back with palms flat on the mat spread on the floor.
- Inhale deep and raise the right leg as high as comfortable. Keep it straight with foot relaxed.
- Hold the left leg straight on the floor. Retain the breath and hold the posture for about 5 seconds.
- Lower the leg slowly and exhale gently.
- Repeat the same on left leg as well.

Uttanpadasana

Repetitions: Increase this practice up to 10 rounds. Later, practise with both legs lifted together. Your stomach gets perfectly strong if you practise holding the Uttanpadasana for one and a half minute.

For perfect results, Uttanpadasana may be repeated raising the legs to progressive heights at 30, 45 and 60 degrees respectively in each round.

7. Sarpasana

- Lie down on your stomach. Spread your arms to your front side.
- Stretch your legs to back side keeping them together like the tail of a snake.
- Bring the palms and elbows close to your ribs so that palms rest under the shoulder.

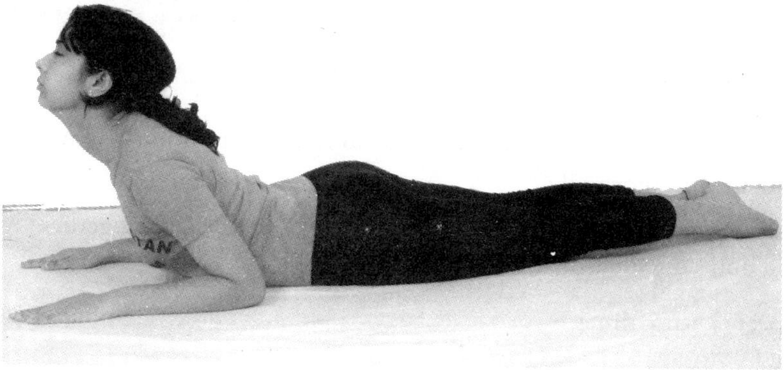

Sarpasana

- Bring the forehead on the floor, keep your eyes closed and face absolutely calm.
- Inhale while lifting up the face with the strength of your spinal column like a snake.
- Ensure no wrinkles at all and bear a cheer on your face.
- Hold the position for comfortable duration.
- Come down to floor gently, exhale, relax and breathe normally. You may rest your arms like a pillow under your face to relax better.

Repetitions: Repeat 3 to 5 times in the same sequence.

8. Sarvangasana

In yoga therapy, Sarvangasana is a cure to **diabetes, asthma, colitis, impotence, thyroid disorders, prolapse, hydrocele, leucorrhoea, menopause** and **menstrual problems.** Rhythmic abdominal breathing during this asana provides a soothing massage onto abdominal organs and releases the normal gravitational pressure from anal muscles and gives ample blood supply to heart, face and brain and tones the legs and reproductive organs. Pressing the chest against the chin (Jalandhar Bandha) stimulates the thyroid gland and works wonderfully to balance the digestive, reproductive, circulatory, nervous and endocrine systems besides supplying enriched blood flow to the brain tranquilising the mind, relieving headache, stress tension, anxiety and fear. Its work on parathyroid gland blesses us with normal growth and regeneration of bones and prevents calcification in joints. The stimulated thymus gland boosts up the immune system. Ailments related to urinary bladder, uterus, painful and irregular menstruation, and even piles and hernia can be cured with practice of Sarvangasana in a proper way. The increased circulation in nerves passing through the neck to brain revitalises the ears, eyes and tonsils and prevents various ear, nose and throat ailments. It may be practised twice a day under observation.

Sarvangasana

- Lie on your back on your mat. Keep the head and spine aligned with straight legs and feet put together. Keep your palms firm on the floor beside the thighs.
- Inhale deep and raise the legs to vertical position with the support of arms.
- Press the palms and arms on the floor to roll the buttocks and spine quite smoothly off the floor.
- Raise the trunk also to a vertical position. Support your back with palms placed behind the ribs. Push the chest gently forward till it presses firmly on the chin.
- Maintain the elbows shoulder wide apart. Ensure that the body is vertical with feet together and in a straight line with the trunk, supported by the shoulders, neck and back of the skull.
- See that the arms continue to balance, the feet are relaxed and the chest rests against your chin.
- Continue to look at the tips of your toes. Hold the final position for a few seconds only in the beginning and increase the time gradually to 3 to 5 minutes.
- On your way back maintain your legs straight at knees and bring feet towards your head. Remove the hands from your back slowly and bring them besides your thighs with palms down.

Repetitions: This asana is practised once for 3 to 5 minutes, but if you are not able to hold position for long in the beginning, then this asana can be repeated 3 to 4 times.

Breathing: Retain breath inside while lifting your legs and rolling the buttocks and spine and while coming back to starting point. Practise slow, deep abdominal breathing when you reach the final position. Lower each vertebrae of the spine gradually to the floor followed by buttocks to resume their vertical position. Hold the knees straight and bring the legs to the floor gently.

Relax in lying position on your back till the heartbeat and respiration are normalised.

Precautions: This asana is prohibited for people suffering from heart diseases, high blood pressure, thrombosis, slipped disc, cervical spondylitis, enlarged thyroid, spleen or liver. It is restricted during menstruation or advanced stage of pregnancy.

9. Halasana

Halasana

- Halasana is ideally practised immediately after Sarvangasana.
- Keep the feet together and straight at knees while lowering the feet slightly over the head from Sarvangasana position until the toes touch the floor but do not force the toes to touch the floor.

- Remove the arms from their position behind the back to rest them on the floor with palms facing down and placed firm on floor. Keep the body relaxed while lowering the legs over the head.
- Maintain this posture beginning from 10 to 15 seconds and add a little per week till it reaches 10 minutes' duration.
- Breathe in while returning to starting position by lowering the back slowly, till the hips touch the ground and the legs reach at right angle. Maintain weight on abdominal muscles and bring the legs gently to starting position with knees straight.

Repetitions: This asana is practised once for 5 to 10 minutes.

Breathing: Inhale and retain breath while lifting both legs using the abdominal muscles. Continue a gentle, rhythmic but still deep breathing when you hold the final position. Hold the breath.

Precautions: This asana is risky to those who suffer from hernia, slipped disc, sodalities, high blood pressure and sciatica. So seek expert advice before making an attempt to do Halasana.

Pranayama

1. Nadishodhan Pranayama

Preparation

- Sit in Padmasana with left leg on right thigh and right leg on left thigh, both knees touching the floor, spine firm and straight. The spine, neck and head should be in straight line.
- Rest your arms comfortably in the lap with relaxed elbows in Brahmanjali Mudra (with left palm resting on right one). Check your posture, it must be firm but relaxed.
- Those who cannot sit in Padmasana may sit in any comfortable meditation posture preferably Siddhasana, Swastikasana or Sukhasana. Under special circumstances, it can be practised sitting with straight back in chair.
- Control the flow of breath with thumb and ring finger of right hand by alternately pressing on the nostril. Index, middle and little finger will remain relaxed and comfortably folded while performing pranayama.

Pranayama

Procedure

Step 1

- Close your eyes and relax yourself with rhythmic yogic breathing for a few minutes.
- Close the right nostril with right thumb. Inhale and exhale through left nostril with perfect awareness and normal respiration rate 5 to 10 times.

- Make sure that there is no sound of air pass while performing this pranayama.
- Now remove pressure of thumb from right nostril and block the flow of breath in left nostril with moderate pressure of the right ring finger.
- Repeat inhalation and exhalation through right nostril as well.

Step 2

- This step has become so popular that some people have given it a separate name as *Anulom Vilom Pranayama.* In this step, we control the duration of inhalation and exhalation with mental count of the holy mantra *OM.*
- Breathe deeply but without strain through left nostril with mental count of holy *OM* keeping the right nostril closed with right thumb.
- Close the left nostril with ring finger and exhale through right nostril with same count.
- Close the right nostril and inhale gently through right nostril with same count and exhale through left nostril in the same manner.
- Avoid forced breathing or rapid counts.
- Practise 10 such rounds. Go on increasing the mental count of mantra gradually with patience until it reaches around 18. After about 40 days of regular practice, start taking more time in exhalation and gradually make it just double of time taken during inhalation.

Step 3

- This step makes it a perfect pranayama, as *Kumbhak* or retention is a must in pranayama. We introduce *Antar Kumbhak* or internal breath retention in this step. Closing the right nostril, inhale very slowly through left one. Close both nostrils and retain the air in lungs for same duration.
- Now exhale smoothly with same length of time as the inhalation.
- As soon as you complete this exhalation, inhale immediately through right nostril keeping the left nostril closed.
- Retain this breath for same duration and exhale through the left.
- The most important thing in this pranayama is the ratio of inhalation, retention and exhalation. As you gain perfect control over ratio of 1 *(Poorak)*: 1 *(Kumbhak)*: 2 *(Rechak),* go on increasing it slowly till it reaches 1:4:2.

2. Bhastrika Pranayama

Preparation

- Sit comfortably in Padmasana, Siddhasana, Swastikasana or any asana of Padmasana group with clean nasal track, eyes gently closed and straight back.
- After obtaining asana, just withdraw awareness from your crossed legs and leave them absolutely free.
- Straighten your spinal column in alignment with neck and head. All the three must look in a single line from back side.
- Now withdraw your awareness from this portion also and observe Gyan Mudra for better concentration, inner joy and firmness in practice. Give both of your index

fingers the shape of a ring and touch their complete nails against bottom part of thumbs, leaving the rest three fingers spread straight. Place the wrists on knees with palms open to sky.

- Now withdraw your awareness from your arms also and leave them absolutely relaxed from shoulder joints.
- Bring your complete awareness to your Manipur Chakra at your navel leaving the chest, face and skull perfectly relaxed.
- Inhale deep and breathe out forcefully through the nose without any strain.
- Repeat it about 10 times, then take a deep breath and breathe out slowly. This is one round. Take about five rounds to clean the nostrils allowing the equal rhythmic flow of breath in both nostrils and be prepared for deep practice of Bhastrika Pranayama.

Procedure

Step 1

- Continue to sit in the same asana.
- Close your right nostril with right thumb. Inhale and exhale forcefully through left nostril 20 times with a snuffing sound in the nose but count each breath mentally.
- During inhalation the diaphragm descends and the abdomen moves outward.
- During exhalation the diaphragm moves upward and the abdomen moves inward.
- After continuing it for five times go on increasing the speed of *Poorak* (inhalation) and *Rechak* (exhalation).
- The increasing speed and force of breath will shorten its depth.
- After about 15 breaths the flow of breath should sound like bellows of a blacksmith where he goes on increasing the fire with repeated force of air pressure.
- The bellows increases the flow of air into the fire and produces more heat. The same way Bhastrika Pranayama produces inner heat in the individual. Perform the pumping action by abdomen without strain.
- Body must be quite still without any jerk.
- Now inhale deep with left nostril only and practise *Antar Kumbhak* (fill the lungs as much as possible) expanding both lungs and the abdomen. Retain the breath and increase *Antar Kumbhak* gradually. Exhale comfortably through left nostril only. Remember inhalation and exhalation must be equal.

Step 2

- Sit in the same position and close the left nostril with ring finger of the right hand.
- Inhale and exhale through right nostril with similar force for 20 times with comfortable posture without jerk.
- Mind that you do not make any extra effort to expand your chest or to lift your shoulders. They must remain as much normal as possible.

- Now inhale deep through right nostril and close both your nostrils retaining breath inside.
- Exhale gently through right nostril only.

Step 3

- Begin with deep, comfortable and rhythmic *Poorak* (inhalation) followed by deep, comfortable and rhythmic *Rechak* (exhalation) with both nostrils together.
- After repeating such breathing for about 20 times, have a deep inhalation, retain the inhaled breath in *Antar Kumbhak* for a comfortable duration.
- With devoted practice, you may go for practising deeper *Antar Kumbhak* (retaining breath in inhaled position) gradually.
- After comfortable *Antar Kumbhak,* go for deep but comfortable exhalation followed by normal breathing.
- In the beginning, you may practise counting numbers during *Antar Kumbhak* to increase the time duration. Later this counting may be replaced with mental chanting of holy mantra for spiritual gains besides good health.
- Twenty times rapid *Poorak Rechak* followed by *Poorak* then *Antar Kumbhak* and finally *Rechak*, this is one round of Bhastrika Pranayama. A beginner can practise five rounds of Bhastrika pranayama every day.
- With growing practice, abdominal bulk is reduced and rectus muscles get stronger. We may increase the number of respirations by 5 per month to a maximum count of 50 through the left, right and both nostrils. In advanced practice, Bhastrika is performed with Mool Bandha and Jalandhar Bandha with *Antar Kumbhak* (internal breath retention).

Precautions: Bhastrika is recommended for people with excellent or normal health. Avoid violent respiration, facial expressions and shaking of body. People with weaker lungs or weaker heart, high blood pressure, hernia, gastric ulcer or epilepsy are advised not to practise Bhastrika Pranayama through magazines or TV programmes. Practitioners are advised to go for a short rest after each round of Bhastrika Pranayama as Bhastrika requires a lot of physical energy. Also it is advisable to take balanced diet, especially milk for risk-free practice of Bhastrika Pranayama.

Bandha

1. Uddian Bandha

- Sit in Padmasana resting right leg on left thigh and left leg on right thigh with soles facing sky.
- Try to touch both your knees to floor and keep the thighs, knees and pelvis relaxed. Maintain your spine, neck and head in a straight line.
- Obtain Gyan Mudra by folding the index fingers to touch the base of the thumbs.
- Keep the other three fingers straight, relaxed and slightly apart and place the wrists on your knees with palms facing upward. Beginners who fail to attain this posture may sit in half lotus or Ardh Padmasana and practise with changed position of feet every day.
- Close the eyes to relax your mind and body.

- Inhale deep through nose only and exhale deep emptying the lungs as much as possible.
- Press down your wrists on the knees and contract the abdominal muscles inward and upward.
- Hold this abdominal lock and hold the breathing out position for as long time as you can without putting any extra strain on your lungs.
- Now relax your wrists and release the Uddian Bandha and allow a slow and deep inhalation.
- Relax until your breathing is normalised then begin the next round.
- You may begin with practice of three to five rounds and gradually increase to ten rounds within a couple of months.

Uddian Bandha

Precautions: In case of ulcer, high blood pressure and heart disease, Uddian Bandha is not recommended. Patients suffering from asthma and hernia are advised to practise Uddian Bandha under expert guidance.

Also remember Uddian Bandha is performed with external breath retention only.

2. Mool Bandha

Stage 1

- Sit in Padmasana (lotus posture) or in Siddhasana (half lotus posture) so that pressure is applied to the perineal region.
- Close the eyes and relax the whole body.
- Be aware of the natural breath for a short while.
- Then focus the awareness on the perineal region.
- Contract this region by pulling up on the muscles of the pelvic floor and then relaxing them.
- Continue to briefly contract and then relax the perineal region as rhythmically and evenly as possible.

Stage 2

- Slowly contract this region and hold the contraction.
- Continue to breathe normally, do not hold the breath.
- Be totally aware of physical sensation.
- Contract a little tighter, but keep the rest of the body relaxed.

- Contract only the muscles related to *mooladhar* (pelvic) region. (In the beginning, the anal and urinary sphincters also contract, but as awareness and control is developed, this will be minimised and eventually will cease. Ultimately the practitioner will feel one point of movement against the heels.)
- Relax the muscles slowly and evenly.
- Adjust the tension in the spine to help focus on the point of contraction.
- Repeat 10 times with maximum contraction and total relaxation.
- An important aspect of yoga that needs to be kept in mind while performing yogasanas, pranayamas and bandhas is that one should never overstretch or put more pressure on the body than it can take.
- Once you ease into the yogic schedule for around 20-30 days, you will be surprised with the flexibility and endurance power that your body will be able to achieve.

Meditation

- Sit in cross-legged position with your back straight and eyes closed. In case you have problem sitting cross-legged on the floor or mat, you can sit straight in the chair.
- Concentrate on whatever you see with closed eyes.
- Let every thought, picture, colour, person etc come and go. Do not indulge yourself in any of the object of your thoughts.
- Try this for 15 to 20 minutes.
- Now think of your divine percept and surrender yourself to Him with a thought that from this moment all your problems are His and He is there to take care of everything. In yoga, it is called '*Ishwar Pranidhan*'.

Nutrition before Pregnancy

Optimum nutrition before pregnancy is important because of the amount of resources childbirth requires. The intake of essential nutrients becomes more important before pregnancy in context of the mother as all the extra nutrition one takes gets stored in the body. This serves as a reserve at the time when the baby is conceived, mainly during first trimester of the pregnancy when the desire to eat is less and whatever one eats comes out as the frequency of throwing up is high. That is when the 'reserves' in the body are of great help to meet the increased nutritional demands. The process of pre-pregnancy nutrition is a process of building up the immune system in preparation of pregnancy and is known as being one of the major benefactors in determining the success rate of conceiving healthy children. Following a nutritionally sound diet before pregnancy can better the chances of a normal birth-weight, improved foetal brain development, and decrease the chances of pregnancy complications. Furthermore, a healthy diet will decrease pregnancy complications in mothers such as anaemia, oedema, morning sickness, fatigue and constipation.

So, start taking a balanced diet which is low in fat and rich in proteins, carbohydrates, vitamin and minerals. Regular Vitamin B_{12} intake is known to reduce the chances of infertility and ill health. It is advisable for a woman planning a baby to take approximately 400 milligrams of folic acid every day. Cereals are rich source of folic acid.

Fathers to be, should also take balanced nutritious diet as healthy eating boosts the fertility levels. Add a lot of proteins, vitamins and minerals, especially Vitamin C as it cuts the risk of damaged sperms, and Zinc as it complements the semen volume and testosterone levels.

Infertility and Inability to Conceive

After planning your pregnancy for more than six months if you are not able to conceive, then get a thorough medical check up done to find out the exact reason for your inability to conceive. There can be several factors adding to delay in conceiving. At times, couples get very depressed if they are not able to conceive but there is no need to panic or getting depressed because maximum problems impeding conception are curable.

Ensure that you continue to have regular intercourse during your fertile days. Men do not have specific fertile days. They produce sperms throughout their active life. Women, on the other hand, can produce ova available for fertilisation only on specific days which are normally the days 14 to 16 before the onset of menstrual cycle. These fertile days vary from woman to woman depending on the length of their menstrual cycle. It is also important to note that a sperm can survive for around 48 hours after ejaculation and can be available for fertilisation during this period, whereas a matured ovum is normally available for fertilisation for only 24 hours after it is released by the ovaries. It is, therefore, important that a couple has intercourse during the period when ovum is available for fertilisation.

After taking care of the pattern of intercourse if you are still not able to conceive then there can be various reasons to it. Let us have a look at various common reasons that add to infertility and inability to conceive.

1. Weight related problems
2. Stress
3. Menstrual disorder
4. Low sperm count
5. Late planning of pregnancy
6. Retroverted Uterus
7. Polycystic Ovaries

Let us now have a look at all these factors responsible for infertility and also know how and which out of these can be treated with application of yoga and dietetics.

1. Weight Related Problems

A. Obesity or Overweight

Obesity is a state in which there is a generalised accumulation of excess adipose (fat) tissues in the body leading to more than 20% of the desirable body weight. It can be caused due to several reasons such as eating habits, genetic factors, low physical activity, hormonal imbalance and excess intake of alcohol. Overweight women have problems in conceiving. And even if they are able to conceive, they carry increased risk of developing diabetes or hypertension during pregnancy and are more likely to end up having a caesarean section during delivery. Also, you cannot lose weight once pregnant so act before conceiving. Women who are closer to their optimal body weight are in a position to tolerate pregnancy and delivery better.

In case you have found out during your medical check up that your excess weight is the root cause for you not being able to conceive, do not worry much. Specific yogic workouts along with prescribed dietary regulations will get you in shape and prepare you physically for pregnancy.

Yoga therapy for obesity

For treating obesity through yoga, the yogic postures or asanas are altered. All asanas during obesity should be practised with a faster pace and with quicker repetitions. They are called dynamic yogic exercises. With the help of these asanas, the energy consumption in the body is increased, which leads to quick and safe weight loss. These asanas need to be performed in the order mentioned below ideally twice a day in the morning and evening before meals.

1. Sarvang Pushti

- Stand straight with your feet together and palms on your thighs.
- Open your feet apart equally to the broadness of your shoulders. While inhaling take both your arms straight above your head and cross them with each other.
- Now exhale and bend downwards in exact position in such a way that your head will be in between your knees.
- Start moving clockwise while inhaling giving your waist the maximum stretch, come back to the position of your head between your knees while exhaling.
- Again repeat the same movement anti-clockwise then clockwise. Do 6 repetitions this way.
- Now while inhaling come back to the upright position, with your hands crossed above your head as in second step.
- While exhaling, come back to the first position you started with, i.e. palms on your thighs and your feet together.
- This is one round. Perform 3 to 5 such rounds.

2. Surya Namaskar

(Mentioned in Pre-Pregnancy on page no. 20)

3. Katichakrasana

(Mentioned in Pre-Pregnancy on page no. 23)

4. Dynamic Sarpasana

(Same as Sarpasana mentioned in 'Pre-Pregnancy' on page no. 26)

Note: In Dynamic Sarpasana, you inhale and exhale forcefully as compared to the normal and gentle breathing in Sarpasana.

5. Uttanpadasana

(Mentioned in Pre-Pregnancy on page no. 25)

6. Dynamic Halasana

- Lie flat on the back with the legs and feet together. Place the arms beside the body with the legs and feet together.
- Place the arms beside the body with the palms facing down.
- While breathing in forcefully raise both the legs to the vertical position, keeping them straight and together using only the abdominal muscles press down on the arms and dynamically lift the buttocks, rolling the back away from the floor. Lower the legs over the head. Try to touch the floor behind the head.

Halasana

- Return to the starting position while exhaling. Again without stopping yourself carry on the third point and repeat the asana 10 to 12 times.
- After completing one round, relax with your legs wide apart.

7. Bhastrika Pranayama

(Mentioned in Pre-Pregnancy on page no. 29)

Diet therapy for obesity

- First step towards reducing weight is to make up your mind that you have to reduce.
- Second step is to develop your liking for low calorie foods.
- Thirdly avoid emotional eating, nibbling between meals and fad diets.

Dietary modifications for obesity

Calories

Cutting down the calories is the first principle for reducing. About thousand calorie diet per day is recommended.

Proteins

Protein intake should be slightly higher than the normal as it gives a feeling of fullness and helps in maintaining good nutritional status. Approximately 20% of the energy is provided by the proteins.

Fats

Some amount of fat is important to make the food acceptable and for the supply of essential fatty acids which play important role in the functions of body. About two to three teaspoons of fats or oils is recommended. Keep in mind that only 15% to 20% of the total energy should be provided by the fats. Foods rich in high fat content should be restricted.

Carbohydrates

Rest of the energy requirement of the body, i.e. 60% to 65% should be provided by the carbohydrates. Carbohydrates are important in the diet during obesity for one more special reason that the dietary fibre present in them helps in giving a feeling of fullness with a lesser amount of calories. Sugar-rich foods like jam, squash, syrups and table sugar should be restricted.

Vitamins and Minerals

To maintain good nutritional status, the reducing diet should contain adequate amounts of minerals and vitamins. Including foods like green leafy vegetables, fresh fruits and whole grain cereals and sprouts in the diet will provide essential amounts of vitamins and minerals.

Foods to be restricted in diet for obesity

- High fat foods like butter, processed cheese, chocolates, creams, ice creams, pastries and fried foods like *samosa, kachori,* patties etc.
- High carbohydrate foods such as breads, cakes, dried fruits, potatoes, sugar, jams etc.
- Carbonated and malted beverages, alcohol and sweetened fruit juices
- Salt content in the food should be minimised as salts are responsible for weight gain in the form of water retention

Special 40-day diet plan

Here we are giving you a special diet plan which, if followed strictly along with the yoga therapy, will reduce 10-12 kilograms of your body weight in 40 days.

MEAL	MENU		
	Exchange 1	*Exchange 2*	*Exchange 3*
Early Morning	Warm water with lemon	Warm water with lemon	Warm water with lemon
Breakfast	Poha (1 small plate), skimmed milk without sugar (200 grams)	Idli (2 in number) sambhar, tea without sugar	Cornflakes in skimmed milk (200 grams) without sugar
Lunch	Sprouted moong dal salad, Bottle gourd cooked in tomato gravy, curd made from skimmed milk, two chapattis	Green salad, masoor dal, curd, two chapattis	Tossed salad in low fat mustard sauce, tinda cooked in onion tomato gravy, curd, two chapattis
Tea Time	One seasonal fruit (except banana, chiku and mango), tea or coffee of skimmed milk without sugar	One seasonal fruit (except banana, chiku and mango), tea or coffee of skimmed milk without sugar	One seasonal fruit (except banana, chiku and mango), tea or coffee of skimmed milk without sugar
Dinner	Tomato soup, peas, cauliflower, vegetable salad, 2 chapattis, one apple	Clear vegetable soup, mix vegetable, salad, 2 chapattis	Cabbage soup, spinach cottage cheese (made from skimmed milk) vegetable, salad, 2 chapattis

Points to ponder

- No sugar and fat content should be added to the food. Vegetables or pulses should be simply cooked in a microwave oven or in a non-stick pan without oil. You can try cooking them in tomato puree.
- You can make your food spicy.

- Reduce sodium intake in your diet (use less salt while cooking).
- If you feel like having something sweet you can have 1 teaspoon of honey (once a day).
- You can have plenty of lemon, tomatoes and onion in your diet without any restriction.
- After completing this diet plan for 40 days, put yourself on weight maintenance diet until you get pregnant. And do not forget to continue the yogic exercises mentioned under yoga before pregnancy.
- If you are more than 15 kilograms overweight even after completing one cycle of this plan, keep yourself on weight maintenance diet for 10 days and again start with one more cycle of the diet plan.

B. Underweight

Does your medical checkup reveal that you being underweight is the reason for you not being able to conceive? Do not worry, we will help you reach your optimal body weight and provide your body with all the nutrients in the prescribed quantity through yoga and diet therapy.

Being underweight can be described as a condition when the body weight is 10% to 20% less than the average weight according to a person's height and sex. There can be several causes for being underweight, such as poor selection of food, irregular eating habits, hyperactive, stressful and tense lifestyle, irregular sleep cycles, weak liver, low appetite etc. Weight loss may also take place as a result of severe infections, prolonged suffering from disease, high fevers, hormonal imbalance and gastrointestinal disturbances. Underweight women face problems in conceiving and are more likely to give birth to underweight, premature babies. Underweight women more often have deficiency of nutrients, which play an important role in preparing the body for pregnancy. It is due to this reason that underweight women face problems in conceiving. So it is important to get as close as possible to your optimal weight before conception.

Yoga therapy for underweight

There are specific yogic techniques that will help you gain weight quickly than you could otherwise have. These techniques will help in increasing your appetite and will aid in building your body mass. Simultaneously these will help in toning up your body and provide your body with more muscle and endurance power.

1. Paschimottanasana

(Mentioned in Pre-Pregnancy on page no. 22)

2. Mayurasana

- Kneel on the floor.
- Place the feet together and separate the knees on the floor with the fingers pointing towards the feet. The hand position will have to be adjusted according to comfort and flexibitily.

- Bring the elbows and forearms together.
- Lean further forward and rest the abdomen on the elbows and the chest on the upper arms.

Mayurasana

- Stretch the legs backwards so that they are straight and together.
- Tense the muscles of the body and slowly elevate the trunk and legs so that they are horizontal to the floor.
- Hold the head upwards.
- The whole body should now be balanced only on the palms of the hands.
- Try to elevate the legs and feet higher, keeping them straight by applying more muscular effort and by adjusting the balance of the body.
- Do not strain.
- In the final position, the weight of the body should be supported by the muscles of the abdomen and not the chest.
- Maintain the pose for a short period of time then slowly return to the base position.
- This is one round. Practise 5 such rounds. The asana should be repeated when the breathing rate has returned to normal.

Breathing: Exhale while raising the body from the floor. Inhale while lowering the body back to the floor. Hold the breath out in the final position.

3. Bakasana

- Squat on the floor with both feet apart.
- Balance on the toes and place the hands flat on the floor directly in front of the feet, with the fingers pointing forward. The eyebrows should be slightly bent.
- Lean forward and adjust the knees so that the inside of the knees touch the outside of the upper arms as near as possible to the armpits.

- Lean forward further, lifting the feet off the floor, balance on the hands with the knees resting firmly on the upper arms.
- Bring the feet together.
- Focus the gaze at the nose tip.
- Hold the final position as long as it is comfortable.
- Slowly lower the feet to the floor.

Breathing: Retain the breath inside in the final position.

Duration: Either practise holding the pose for once for 2 to 3 minutes or practise raising and lowering the feet several times.

Bakasana

4. Matsyasana

- Sit in Padmasana and relax the whole body.
- Carefully bend backward, supporting the body with the arms and elbows.
- Lift the chest slightly, take the head back, and lower the crown of the head to the floor.
- Hold the big toes and rest the elbows on the floor.
- Adjust the position of the head so that the maximum arch of the back is attained.
- Relax the arms and hold the body, allowing the head and the buttocks and leg to support the weight of the body.

Matsyasana

- Close the eyes and breathe slowly and deeply.
- Return to the starting position, reversing the order of movements.

Breathing: Breathe deeply and slowly in the final position.

Duration: The final position should be held for 3 to 5 minutes.

5. Shavasana

- Lie flat on the back with the arms about 15 centimetres away from the body, palms facing upwards.
- A thin pillow or folded cloth may be placed behind the head to prevent discomfort. Let the fingers curl up slightly.
- Move the feet slightly apart to a comfortable position and close the eyes.
- The head and spine should be in a straight line.
- Make sure that the head does not fall on one side or the other.
- Relax the whole body and stop all physical movement.
- Become aware of the natural breath and allow it to become rhythmic and relaxed.
- Begin to count the breaths from 27 backwards to 0.
- If the mind wanders and the next number is forgotten, bring it back to the counting and start again at 27.
- Physical awareness should be on relaxing the whole body and the spiritual awareness should be on *ajna chakra.*

Duration: This asana should be practised for 10 to 20 minutes.

6. Gyan Mudra

- Assume a comfortable meditation posture. Make sure that your spine is erect.
- Fold the index fingers so that they touch the inside root of the thumbs. Straighten the other three fingers of each hand so that they are relaxed and slightly apart.
- Place the hands on the knees with the palms facing down.
- Close the eyes and relax the arms and hands.
- Sit in the posture for 5 to 10 minutes.

7. Bhramri Pranayama

- Sit in any comfortable meditation asana. The spinal cord should be erect, the head straight and the hands resting on the knees in Gyan Mudra.
- The ideal posture for this practice is Padamasana.
- Close the eyes and relax the whole body for a short time. The lips should remain gently closed with the teeth slightly separated throughout the practice. This allows the sound vibrations to be heard and felt more distinctly in the brain. Make sure that the jaws are relaxed.
- Raise the arms sideways and bend the elbows, bringing the hands to ears. Use the index or middle finger to plug the ears (thumb can also be used). The flap of the ears may be pressed without inserting the fingers.

Bhramri Pranayama

- Bring the awareness to the centre of the head, where *ajna chakra* is located, and keep the body absolutely still.
- Breathe in through the nose.
- Exhale slowly and in a controlled manner, while making a deep steady humming sound like that of a black bee.
- The humming sound should be smooth, even and continuous for the duration of the exhalation.
- The sound should be soft and mellow, making the front of the skull vibrate.
- This is one round.
- Now breathe in deeply and repeat the process.

Duration: 5 to 10 rounds are sufficient in the beginning and then slowly increase to 10 to 15 minutes.

Diet therapy for underweight

The diet therapy for underweight people will work better if you continue with your yogic regime during this period.

Dietary modifications

Energy

An underweight person requires more energy than others. Therefore adding 500 extra calories a day will help to gain about one pound a week. If more and quicker weight gain is desired then daily energy intake may be increased by 1000 kilocalories. A 2500 to 3000 calorie diet is recommended for moderately active individuals for effective weight gain.

Fats

We know that fats are concentrated source of energy and give a boost to weight gain but they must be added in a moderate amount so that they partly meet the energy needs but should not exceed the tolerance limits.

Carbohydrates

A high carbohydrate diet is helpful in meeting the energy needs during the treatment of underweight. Fiber intake should not be more than normal because it gives the feeling of fullness resulting in less motivation to eat.

Minerals and Vitamins

There should be sufficient amount of vitamins and minerals in the diet because they help in regaining health.

Other Nutrients

- As an underweight person cannot adjust at once to the high calorie intake in diet, there should be no forced eating and small but frequent meals should be taken.
- Easily digestible protein foods like milk, combination of cereals and pulses should be included in the diet.
- Low fibre carbohydrate foods like sugar, jaggery, honey, cereals, starchy vegetables and fruits are recommended in a day's diet.
- Emulsified fats like butter, cream, and buffalo milk should be included in the diet.
- Plenty of green and yellow vegetables, all types of fruits, sprouted legumes and pulses and whole grain cereals should be added in the diet in order to get an adequate amount of vitamins and minerals.

Special menu plan for underweight

MEAL	MENU		
	Exchange 1	*Exchange 2*	*Exchange 3*
Early Morning	Tea with cookies	Lemon and honey water	Tea with rusk
Breakfast	2 paneer parantha or 2 toasts with omelette and 1 glass whole fat milk	Cornflakes with milk, 2 cheese sandwiches	2 aloo parantha, butter, curd and 1 apple
Mid-morning	Sprouted moong dal, poha (chiwra)	Sprouted chana cooked	Baked kidney beans (rajma)
Lunch	Cowpea (lobia) curry, methi aloo, curd, 2-3 chapattis, ½ cup rice, 1 sweet	Dal (any), palak paneer, curd, 2-3 chapattis, ½ cup rice, 1 sweet	Peas paneer curry, beans potato vegetable, 2-3 chapattis, curd, ½ cup rice, 1 sweet
Tea Time	Almond milkshake, vermicelli cooked with mix vegetables	Banana milkshake, aloo poha	Chiku milkshake, sweet potato or lotus stem chat
Dinner	Dal (any), cabbage potato vegetable, 2-3 chapattis, ½ cup rice/ pulao, carrot kheer	Rajma curry, cauliflower potato vegetable, 2-3 chapattis, ½ cup rice/ biryani, suji kheer	Chhole curry, mix vegetables, 2-3 chapattis, ½ cup rice (boiled or fried), makhana kheer

This menu plan is specially designed for underweight non-pregnant as well as pregnant women. All the food exchanges are also given keeping in mind that food should not become monotonous.

This diet plan followed strictly with yoga therapy will help you in gaining 5-8 kg of weight in a month.

2. Stress

Stress has affected virtually everyone from a pre-school child to adolescent children, from young working women to housewives to women past middle age, from men dealing with day-to-day pressures in their jobs to the elderly people getting adjusted to their retirements and changed lifestyles. Stress penetrates deep into the psyche and leaves a person with muscular, nervous, digestive, glandular, respiratory, cardiovascular and even blood circulation disorders. Stress has been identified as the biggest responsible factor for the decrease in the levels of testosterone and low sperm count. On the other hand, in females the stress affects the glandular system resulting in disturbed menstruation cycle responsible for inability to conceive. We are going to eliminate stress completely from our lives by learning few simple yogic techniques and dietary modifications. Today, yoga is perhaps the only solution to the ever increasing problem of stress.

Yoga therapy for stress

Yoga creates a climate of dynamic peacefulness and harmony within. This relaxing and rejuvenating experience removes us from involvement with the stressors. Yogic postures do a balancing act on the different systems of the body by slowing down the mental activity and by gently stretching the body and massaging the internal organs. By practising yoga on a regular basis, people are said to have built up a natural response to stress and bring the relaxed state more and more into their daily lives. So make up your mind that you will get rid of stress.

1. Tadasana

(Mentioned in Pre-Pregnancy on page no. 19)

2. Micro Exercise for *Kapal* (Brain)

Step 1

- Stand straight on your asana with feet together. Keep your mouth closed, set your head comfortably relaxed and bend your head back.
- Keep the eyes open to sky. Bring your awareness to *Shikha Kshetra* (the middle portion of head where *Pandits* have their *shikha* or *choti*).
- Inhale deeply with pressure till you feel the grip at *shikha* and the surrounding area.
- Exhale gently and repeat the process 10 to 20 times. Relax your head with feet open wide.

Step-1

Step 2

- Close your feet again and stand straight with relaxed neck.
- Look at a distance equal to your height from your toes.
- Hold this position and concentrate on the top tender part of your head known as *Brahma Randhra*.
- Inhale deeply to feel the *Brahma Randhra* gripped through the pressure of your inhalation.
- Repeat 10 to 20 times and relax yourself.

Step 3

- Join your feet together and stand straight again with tension-free back and shoulders.
- Set your neck perfectly loose and fix your chin at *Kanth Kupeh* just at the centre of collarbone joint at the bottom of neck.
- Concentrate over the last end of skull at deep part over the back of your neck. Have deep and forceful inhalation leading to maximum grip of control over the medulla.
- Exhale gently and repeat it 10 to 20 times followed by perfect relaxation. Set your head relaxed, breathing in normal rhythm.

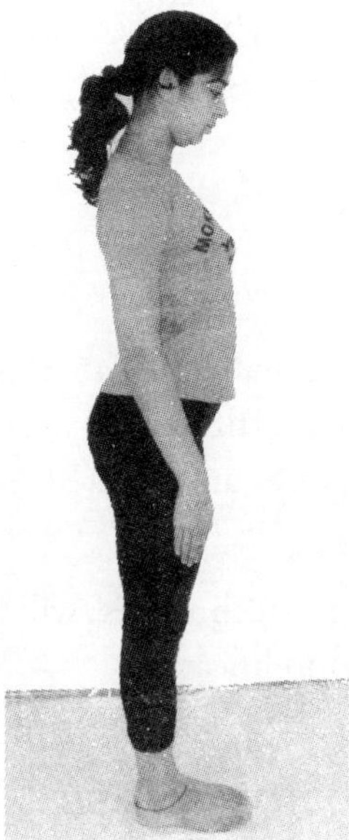

Step-2

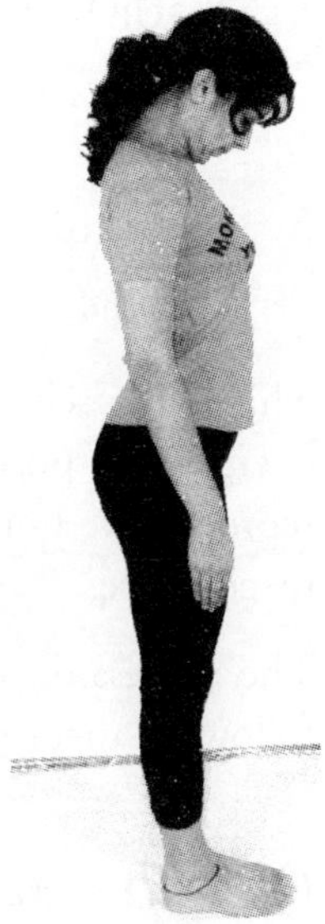

Step-3

3. Singhasana

- Sit on your practice mat in kneeling position on your toes put together and heels wide apart with knees about two feet apart.
- Lean a little forward with arch on lower back, chest lifted up and maximum stretch on front side of the neck.
- Place the palms on the floor between your knees with fingers pointing towards body. Keep your arms perfectly straight and rest the body on straight arms.
- Focus your eyes at the eyebrow centre. (In yoga, it is called *Shyambhavi Mudra*).
- Inhale deeply and open your mouth wide, allowing the tongue to extend outward to the maximum.
- Now produce a clear and steady roar (*Singh Garjana*) of the lion from the throat keeping mouth wide open.
- Close your mouth and inhale with nose again.

Repetition: Repeat the above mentioned steps 5 times.

Singhasana

4. Nadishodhan Pranayama

   (Mentioned in Pre-Pregnancy on page no. 28)

5. Meditation

   (Mentioned in Pre-Pregnancy on page no. 33)

This short schedule will take 45 minutes to 1 hour of your day and will provide the optimum energy and positive attitude to deal with every situation in life. Once you are de-stressed, the reproductive hormones are secreted in right quantities by the body and you become better prepared to conceive.

The aforesaid yogic techniques will become even more effective when practised along with the following dietary modifications:

Diet therapy for stress

The diet during stress should be such that it has ingredients which are known to suppress the bio-chemical changes causing stress. Emotional eating or eating too much should be consciously avoided. Researches prove that people who eat natural foods, whole grain cereals, jaggery instead of sugar, whole fruits, seasonal fresh raw vegetables are less prone to stress than those who have irregular diet cycles and eat fad diets.

Dietary modifications

Vitamins and Minerals

All vitamins are important but Vitamin C or ascorbic acid plays an important role in release of the two hormones – epinephrine and norepinephrine from the adrenal glands of the body. These hormones help the body to deal with stressful situations like day-to-day tensions, stresses of infections and injury also.

Vitamins B is also of great importance in outwitting stress, especially B_1 (thiamine) is necessary for boundless energy. In minerals, iron takes the first bench in importance. Functions of iron are fascinating in context of stress. Iron plays an important role in maintenance of specific brain functions like immediate memory, capacity to learn and attention span. Good amount of iron consumed helps in eradicating mental stress. The other specific functions of iron include transport of oxygen and oxidation of carbohydrates, fats and proteins within the cells thus releasing the locked energy. This energy is required in dealing with physical and mental stress. Green leafy vegetables, cereals, pulses especially whole ones and soyabean contain good amounts of iron.

Things to remember

- Other nutrients should be taken in right amounts according to the recommended dietary allowances.
- Avoid oily, fried and high sodium (salty) foods.
- Avoid tea, coffee and alcohol.
- Avoid onion and garlic in your diet the day you feel depressed or stressed.
- Add vegetable juice (carrot, spinach, beetroot, bottle gourd, cucumber, celery) and fresh fruit juice in your diet (no canned juices with added sugar, only natural fruit juices).
- Stick to vegetarian diet as far as possible.

3. Menstrual Disorder

Irregularities in the menstruation cycle are mainly caused by hormonal imbalance. Two main sex hormones, oestrogen and progesterone, play an important role in the control of menstrual cycle. These sex hormones come under the influence of pituitary gland. Abnormal hormonal regulation leads to the menstrual disorder. Ovulation is a pre-requisite for getting pregnant. In women with regular menstrual cycles of 28-35 days, ovulation takes place once every cycle. However, some women may have erratic menstrual cycles (often getting periods 3-4 times a year or even less) due to the menstrual disorders. This means that they have fewer chances of getting pregnant not only because they have fewer possible fertile periods, but also because they may not be ovulating in every cycle. (Note that ovulation does not necessarily take place in every menstrual cycle).

If you identify yourself with this problem and are unable to conceive, yoga and dietetics is there for you to get your menstrual cycle in order.

Yoga therapy in menstrual disorders

It is important to note while performing *yogasanas* for menstrual disorders that these are to be performed during normal days as *yogasanas* are not recommended during menstrual periods.

1. Paschimottanasana

(Mentioned in Pre-Pregnancy on page no 22)

2. Baddh Padmasana

- Sit comfortably on your yoga mat with your legs spread on front side.
- Fold the left leg at knee and rest it on the root of right thigh.
- Now fold the right leg and rest it on the root of left thigh.
- Make it comfortable to rest the knees on floor. Balance on your sit bones and hold the spine, neck and head in straight single line position.
- Try to bring your heels still closer to each other under the navel (at *Kand Kshetra*).

- Let the soles be wrapped around lower abdomen so that the right toe could be gripped with right hand and the left toe could be gripped with left hand easily from behind.
- Hold this locked position with back straight and chest high.
- Release tension from all body parts. Keep your face calm.
- Enjoy rhythmic breathing.

Baddh Padmasana

Repetition: This Baddh Padmasana must be repeated with changed position of legs and arms for 3 to 5 times. Try each position once for 3 minutes.

3. Sarpasana

(Mentioned in Pre-Pregnancy on page no. 26)

4. Chakrasana

- Ensure that the mat does not slip and lie down on your back folding the knees with heels touching the buttocks.
- Place the palms on floor beside your head fingers pointing towards the shoulders.
- Now inhale and raise the body up making an arch as high as possible on your spinal column.
- Gradually practise moving the arms and feet still closer to each other.
- Maintain perfect pose as long as possible. Rest the head on floor and then lower the rest of body.

Chakrasana

Repetition: Repeat the process 3 to 5 times.

Breathing: Inhale in the starting position. Hold your breath while raising your body up. Breathe rhythmically in the final position and exhale after lowering the body.

5. Dhanurasana

- Lie flat on the stomach with the legs and feet together, and the arms and hands beside the body.
- Bend the knees and bring the heels close to the buttocks.
- Clasp the hands along the ankles.
- Place the chin on the floor.
- This is the starting position.
- Tense the leg muscles and push the feet away from the body. Arch the back, lifting the thighs, chest and hand together.

- Keep the arms straight.
- In the final position, the head is tilted back and the abdomen supports the entire body on the floor.
- The only muscular contraction is in the legs, the back and the arms remain relaxed.
- Hold the final position for as long as comfortable and then slowly relaxing the leg muscles, lower the legs, chest and head to the starting position.
- Release the pose and relax in the prone position until the respiration returns to normal.

Dhanurasana

Repetition: This is one round. Practise 3 to 5 rounds.

Breathing: Inhale deeply in the starting position. Retain the breath while raising the body. Retain the breath inside in the final position or practise slow, deep breathing so that the body rocks gently in unison with the breath. Exhale while returning in the prone position.

6. Shalabhasana

- Lie flat on stomach with the legs and feet together and the soles of feet stretched.
- The arms may be placed either under the body or by the sides, with the palms downwards or the hands clenched.
- Stretch the chin slightly forward and rest it on the floor throughout the practice.
- Close the eyes and relax the body. This is the starting position.
- Slowly raise the legs as high as possible, keeping them straight and together.
- The elevation of the legs is produced by applying pressure with the arms against the floor and contracting the lower back muscles.
- Hold the final position for as long as is comfortable without strain.
- Slowly lower the legs to the floor.
- Return to the starting position and relax the body with the head turned to one side.
- Allow the respiration and heartbeat to return to normal.

Repetition: Up to 5 rounds when performed dynamically. Up to 3 rounds when performed statically.

Breathing: Inhale deeply in the starting position. Retain the breath while raising and holding the position. Exhale while lowering the legs. Beginners may find it helpful to inhale while raising the legs.

7. Uddian Bandha

(Mentioned in Pre-Pregnancy on page no. 31)

Dietary modifications

Proteins

The glands are made up of proteins and their secretions are also proteins. The hormones go directly into the bloodstream and are important directors of all chemical processes of the entire body. As we know that the biggest factor responsible for menstrual disorders is hormonal imbalance, therefore, the main nutrient 'protein' comes out as main area of consideration in the diet. A proper intake of proteins should be taken. Good quality protein-rich foods like fortified milk and milk products, especially cottage cheese and *khoya*, soyabeans, pulses and legumes should be added to the diet. Non-vegetarians can add eggs and meat as they have good quality proteins but they should keep in mind that with yogic schedule we ask people to avoid taking non-vegetarian diet and stick to pure vegetarian *satvik* diet.

Vitamins and Minerals

Adequate minerals and vitamins are also necessary to maintain a healthy balance in the functioning of your glands. All vitamins are important but those of B family are of greater importance. Addition of wheat germ, yoghurt, milk, sprouted and fermented foods, nuts and oilseed, leafy green and yellow vegetables, citrus fruits in daily diet will fulfil the demands of vitamins.

Other Nutrients

Carbohydrates and fats should be added in the diet according to the daily requirement (R.D.A.) of the individual.

4. Low Sperm Count (Males)

Now days low sperm count has become one of the major factors adding to delay in conceiving. Few factors resulting in low sperm count are obesity, stress, erratic diet lacking nutrients, intake of alcohol, smoking etc. Though medication helps in increasing the sperm count for a short period, yoga has shown miraculous results in this matter. Yoga combined with proper modifications in diet can do wonders for the males suffering with this particular problem in the long term. While practising yoga especially in this regard one has to avoid alcohol, smoking, non-vegetarian diet patterns, tea and coffee. If you cannot restrict tea completely then you can have one or two cups of tea during the day.

Yoga therapy for low sperm count

Yoga creates a suitable environment for better functioning of reproductive organs and help increase sperm count. This is possible as yoga impacts all the physiological and biochemical processes that aid in the proliferation of sperms.

1. Ardha Matsyendrasana

Ardha Matsyendrasana

- Sit comfortably on your mat with feet together and legs spread.
- Fold your left leg and bring the heel and sole close to right side allowing left hand to hold the right toe.
- Move your right arm towards your back till it touches the left side of lower abdomen.
- Move your face to right side and allow your chin and left side of cheek to touch the right shoulder.
- Continue normal but deep rhythmic breathing. Hold the position for about 25 breaths.

Repetitions: Repeat the same cycle on another side also. This was one round. Practise 5 such rounds.

2. Chakrasana

Chakrasana

(Mentioned under 'Yoga therapy in menstrual disorders' on page no. 50)

3. Gupta Padmasana

- Assume Padmasana.
- Place the hands on the floor in front of the knees. leaning on the arms, raise the buttocks and stand on the knees.
- Slowly lower the front side of the body to the floor in the prone position.
- Rest either the chin or the cheek on the floor.
- Place the palms together behind the back.
- The fingers may point downward or upward in *namaskar* position.

- Close the eyes and relax the whole body.
- Return to the starting position, cross the legs the other way and repeat the asana.
- Hold the position as long as is comfortable.

Breathing: normal and unrestrained in the final position.

4. Sarvangasana

(Mentioned in Pre-Pregnancy on page no. 26)

5. Halasana

(Mentioned in Pre-Pregnancy on page no. 27)

6. Shirshasana

Step 1
- Sit in Vajrasana, close the eyes and relax the whole body.
- After a few minutes, open the eyes, bend forward and place the forearms on a folded blanket with the fingers interlocked and the elbows in front of knees.
- The distance between the elbows should be equal to the distance from each elbow to the interlocked fingers, forming an equilateral triangle.
- Place the crown of the head on the blanket between the interlocked fingers. Wrap the hands around the head to make a firm support so that it cannot roll backward when pressure is applied.

Step 2
- Lift the knees and buttocks off the floor and straighten the legs.

Step 3
- Slowly walk the feet as close as possible towards the trunk and head, gradually moving the back towards the vertical position.
- Bend the knees slightly; press the thighs against the abdomen and lower chest.
- Transfer the body weight slowly from the toes onto the head and arms, maintaining the steady balance.
- Raise one foot off the floor about 20 centimetres carefully balance, then raise the other foot and balance on the head and arms.

Step 4
- Bending the knees, gradually raise the calves in a controlled movement.
- Adjust the trunks slightly to counter-balance the weight of the legs.

Shirshasana

- Fold the legs back to the heels and move towards the buttocks. To accomplish this movement, contract the muscles of the lower back. The knees are now pointing down with the legs together.
- Maintain the position for a few seconds, being aware of complete balance before proceeding.

Step 5
- Raise the knees to the vertical position. Keeping the heels near the buttocks, slowly straighten the hips so that the thighs move up and away from the torso.
- Raise the knees until they point directly upward and the thighs are in line with the trunk.
- Balance the body.

Step 6
- Slowly straighten the knees and raise the calves.
- The whole body should be in one straight line with the feet relaxed. This is the final position.
- Close the eyes and balance the whole body, relaxing in the final position for as long as is comfortable.

Step 7
- Return to the starting position.
- Slowly bend the knees and lower the body with the control in the reverse order until the toes touch the floor.
- Remain with the head on the ground in the kneeling position for a short time, and then slowly return to the upright position.

Rest: After practising asanas, lie down on the yoga mat and relax your body in Shavasana for 10 minutes.

Repetitions: This posture is practised once. Beginners should start by holding the position for 30 seconds gradually adding about 1 minute per week. Finally it should be practised for 3 to 5 minutes.

Breathing: Inhale at the end of step 1. Retain the breath inside while raising the body into the final position. Beginners may practise normal breathing while coming into the posture. Breathe normally in the final position.

7. Nadishodhan Pranayama

(Mentioned in Pre-Pregnancy on page no. 28)

8. Uddian Bandha

(Mentioned in Pre-Pregnancy on page no. 31)

9. Moola bandha

(Mentioned in Pre-Pregnancy on page no. 32)

Diet Therapy for Low Sperm Count

The testes are the main male organs of generation where spermatozoa are produced and the male sex hormone testosterone is produced. This hormone is secreted by the interstitial cells under the stimulation of the Luteinizing Hormone (LH) of the pituitary. Therefore the main area of concern in the diet therapy for low sperm count is the proper functioning of pituitary and sex glands, so that proper amount of semen is produced. A basic well-balanced diet should be taken.

Dietary Modifications

Proteins

As we have read earlier during the diet therapy for irregular menstruation, the glands are made up of proteins and their secretions are also proteins. The hormones go directly into the bloodstream and are important directors of all chemical processes of the entire body. As we know that the biggest factor responsible for low sperm count is hormonal imbalance, the main nutrient protein comes out as the main area of consideration in the diet. A high intake of proteins should be taken. On a high protein diet, restoration of sexual potency and marked increase in sperm count are quickly regained. Good quality protein-rich foods like fortified milk, and milk products especially cottage cheese and *khoya*, soyabeans, green leafy vegetables and pulses and legumes should be consumed.

Vitamins and Minerals

All vitamins especially folic acid, pantothenic acid and para-aminobenzoic acid present in vitamin B are important for glandular health. Add curd in your daily diet as curd bacillus has the ability to synthesise the B vitamins in the intestines. Vitamin A is needed for the health of the prostate and controls the rhythm of the sexual cycle. Deficiency of this vitamin can cause marked reduction in fertility and disturbed sexual behaviour. Vitamin E is needed for the formation of sperm. It shows a marked effect on the sex glands and is essential for the good health of testicles. Severe deficiencies of this vitamin can result in lack of interest in sex and impotency in the males. With the deficiencies in iron and vitamin C, sexual inactivity develops. Zinc plays an important role in this regard as it complements the semen volume and testosterone levels. Calcium deficiency has the same effect as that of protein deficiency. Addition of whole cereals, wheat germ, yogurt, sprouted and fermented foods, nuts and oilseed, leafy green and yellow vegetables, citrus fruits are necessary in daily diet to fulfil the demands of vitamins and minerals.

Other Nutrients

Carbohydrates and fats should be added in the diet according to the daily requirement (R.D.A.) of the individual.

5. Late Planning of Pregnancy

More and more women today have become as much career-oriented as men. Increasing professionalism and a quest for improved lifestyles have led to both husband and wife working to earn livelihood. This has resulted in a more empowered, confident and independent womenfolk. The flip side of this transformation in the social canvas is that couples often find it difficult to plan for family at the right age. They prefer to settle down professionally and financially before they make up their mind to start a family. And by that time they often find themselves in mid-thirties. For a woman over the age of 35, conceiving becomes a problem. Infertility increases with age. Fertility peaks for both sexes in their mid-twenties and then appears to decline steadily in women over thirty and men over forty. Tubal infections, fibroid tumors and endometriosis are more common in older women and are a common cause for infertility.

Regular practice of yoga as mentioned in the pre-pregnancy section and a diet rich in nutrients needed for vitality indicated in the same section can help to a great extent in late planning of pregnancy. The results during the old age pregnancy may take longer time to show up than in others.

6. Retroverted Uterus

The normal position of a uterus is that of facing forward, however many women are born with their uteruses facing backward (retroverted) instead of forward. This condition can be diagnosed either by a gynaecologist, or through an ultrasound. One simple way to compensate for this problem of a retroverted uterus is for the woman to lie on her stomach after intercourse. (Women with regular uteruses who are planning to get pregnant are asked to lie on their backs and lift their legs from their hips after sex in order to improve the chances of fertilisation). If retroverted uterus is the only problem, then in most cases the woman will conceive. However, if she still does not get pregnant, then the doctor may advise surgery.

7. Polycystic Ovaries

Cysts are formed when the follicle fails to rupture at the time of ovulation and begins to grow instead. This condition occurs due to hormonal imbalance and is marked by absent or infrequent menstruation. Women having this condition have a chronic tendency to have their periods at intervals ranging from every six weeks to six months. Conception becomes difficult due to irregular ovulation. This problem can only get cured with medical assistance mainly by a s mall surgery.

The above mentioned are the common reasons for women being unable to conceive. And most of these problems can be cured or treated with the help of yoga and dietetics. The important point to be kept in mind though is not to worry too much and not to think about getting pregnant all the time.

Understanding Pregnancy

Pregnancy is a prime differentiating experience among all experiences for a woman during her entire lifetime. This wonderful experience is so different from any other stage in a woman's life that it ought to be understood for what it is and what it encompasses. Simply put, following are the stages in a normal pregnancy.

Ovulation

The ovaries are two almond-shaped glands placed one on each side of the uterus. They contain a large number of immature ova (eggs), each one of which is surrounded by a cluster of nutritive follicle cells. At each menstruation cycle, one of these ova begins to mature and develops into a Graffian follicle. When the follicle has matured, it secretes enough estradiol to trigger the acute release of Luteinizing Hormone (LH). In the average cycle of 28 days, this LH surge starts around Day-12 of the cycle and may last 48 hours. The release of LH matures the egg and weakens the wall of the follicle in the ovary. Tension within the follicle leads to its rupture and thus the ovulation takes place. Between 14th to 18th days of menstruation cycle of the woman (Days vary depending upon the length of menstruation cycle. The 14th day is said in context with an average menstrual cycle of 28 days) an ovary releases a ripe egg. The egg is caught by the fingers of the fallopian tube and is taken inside the tube. The egg can survive inside the tube for approximately 24 hours. In some women, ovulation features a characteristic pain called *Mittelschmerz* (German term meaning 'middle pain') which lasts for several hours.

Conception

Conception takes place by the activity of the male and female essential sex organs – the testes and the ovaries – producing male and female sex cells, sperms and ova. When a man reaches orgasm during intercourse, the semen is ejaculated in the woman's vagina from the male sex organ – the penis. This semen contains around 200 to 400 million sperms. Many of them are spilled out or are lost in the way, but some swim through the mucus secreted by the cervix. This cervix becomes thin and stretchy around ovulation and then the sperms cross the womb into the fallopian tube. The sperm can survive in the tube for 48 hours. Sperms carry a substance that can dissolve the outer layer of the egg. In this way, one of them penetrates the egg. When one sperm has entered successfully in the egg, no other sperm can get inside. The sperm loses its tail and its head begins to swell. Now the union of the two cells, the egg of the mother and the sperm of the father, forms a single cell, which later develops into the baby.

The Cell Division

With conception, the cell division starts taking place. The cell starts to divide into more and more number of cells, and travels down the fallopian tube.

Reaching the Womb

Approximately on the fourth day after the fertilisation, the egg reaches the cavity of the womb. Till this time it develops into a ball of about 100 cells called blastocyst, with a hollow fluid-filled centre, but is still small to be seen with the naked eye. For the next few days, it floats about in the womb cavity.

Implantation

The blastocyst gets embedded in the soft, thick lining of the womb at about the end of the week three. This is called implantation. When the egg is securely attached to the lining of the womb, conception is complete. Placenta is formed when sponge like fingers from the outer cells of the embryo start to burrow into the lining, to link up with the mother's blood vessels. Placenta is an organ to which the foetus is attached by the means of an umbilical cord. It is the lifeline of the foetus. Placenta provides nourishment to the growing foetus through the maternal blood. Some of the cells of the foetus develop into the umbilical cord, and the membranes that protect the baby. The inner cells of the foetus divide into three layers, which develop into the different body parts of the baby.

Changes in the Body

Pregnancy is the period when maximum changes take place in the body of a woman. It is also called the period of great physiological stress for the woman. The development of the foetus brings about many physiological, biochemical and hormonal changes in the body of the mother. Let us understand these changes to be able to understand pregnancy and the causes of common discomforts (which women come across in different phases of pregnancy) better and be prepared to cope up with these changes.

Increase in the Basic Metabolic Rate (BMR)

There is a pronounced increase in the BMR due to the foetal growth and development. It rises by about 5% in the first trimester and around 12% in the later stages of pregnancy.

Gastrointestinal Changes

There are marked gastrointestinal changes during pregnancy. Nausea, vomiting and constipation occur due to reduced gastric tone and secretion. The acid and pepsin secretion in the stomach is less and there is regurgitation of the stomach contents in the oesophagus leading to a sensation of heartburn and vomiting. This becomes more pronounced with the increasing pressure of the foetus. In the later stages of the pregnancy, the efficiency of absorption of nutrients increases as a result of natural mechanism of the adaptation to the increased needs of the body. 'PICA' or craving for some particular food and aversion to others observed in pregnant ladies is also a result of gastrointestinal changes.

Hormonal Changes

During pregnancy increased secretion of the growth hormone by the pituitary gland, thyroxin secreted by thyroid gland which regulates metabolism in the body, aldosterone, the salt-conserving hormone by the adrenal gland and parathormone secreted by the parathyroid gland which regulates calcium, phosphorus and magnesium metabolism are noticed.

Changes in the Body Fluid

There is an increase in the blood volume by 40% by the end of the pregnancy. The capacity of the heart to pump blood is increased by abut 33%. The increased amount of blood is required to carry the nutrients to the foetus and take metabolic wastes away from the foetus. With the increase in the blood volume, most of the nutrients carried by the fluids are available to the placenta. Intracellular water also increases in addition to the increase in fluid with the circulatory system. With the increase in blood volume, the concentration of plasma proteins, haemoglobin and other blood constituents is lowered. This is usually a cause of anaemia which is experienced by 60% to 70% of the pregnant women.

Altered Renal Functions

There is an increased production of the various metabolites like creatinine, urea and other waste products due to foetal and maternal metabolism during pregnancy. To facilitate their clearance, the rate of blood flow through kidneys is increased with a subsequent increase in the rate of glomerular filtration in the nephrons.

Developmental Stages of Pregnancy

On the basis of various changes, complications and different stages of foetal development the human pregnancy is divided into three trimesters. Different trimesters bring about different changes and developments in the mother and in the foetus. Human pregnancy lasts approximately 9 calender months between the time of the last menstrual cycle and childbirth (approximately 38 weeks from fertilisation).

The medical term for a pregnant woman is *genetalian*, just as the medical term for the potential baby is *embryo* (early weeks) and then *foetus* (until birth). A woman who is pregnant for the first time is known as a *primigravida*. We shall study more about these three trimesters in the coming sections.

The First Trimester

First trimester covers the developmental period of conception from first to third month of pregnancy (0 to 14 weeks). This is a very sensitive and hazardous period, because the embryo is more likely to suffer injury from outside effects such as jerks, drugs and infections.

By the end of the first three weeks, fertilisation and implantation is completed. Till this time the ovum remains practically unchanged in size because there is a lack of outside source of nourishment but rapid internal development takes place. With implantation, the ovum becomes a parasite. All important external and internal features start to develop after implantation.

Development of Embryo during First Trimester

Foetal Development in the First Month

- The embryo is enclosed within two membranes, the inner amnion and the outer chorion which consist a bag of membranes called the amniotic sac. This is filled with amniotic fluid, which protects the foetus and also allows the free movement and uniform growth of the foetus.
- Embryo develops a brain, spine and central nervous system and four shallow pits appear on the head, which will later become the baby's eyes and ears.
- The embryo has the beginnings of the digestive system, mouth and jaw. The stomach and chest are developing. The heart can be seen as a large bulge at the front of the chest, by the end of the month it starts beating. A system of blood vessels is forming.
- Four tiny limb buds develop and length of the embryo becomes 6 mm (1/4") about the size of an apple seed.

Foetal Development in the Second Month

- Development is very rapid during the second month. By the end of the second month, major body organs and body systems, including the brain, lungs, liver, and stomach begin to develop.
- The first bone cells appear during this time.
- Eyelids form and grow but remain sealed shut. The inner ear is forming. Ankles, toes, wrists, fingers, and sexual organs are developing.
- At the end of the second month of pregnancy, the baby looks like a tiny human infant. If it is a boy, the penis will begin to appear.
- The baby is a little over 1 inch long and still weighs less than 1 ounce.

Foetal Development in the Third Month

- Baby is completely formed by the end of the third month. The fingers and toes are now more distinct and have soft nails. The baby's hands are more developed than the feet and the arms are longer than the legs.
- The head is quite large compared to the rest of its body. Fuzzy hair begins to form on the little one's head. The colour of the hair is white (unpigmented).
- Accessory apparatus placenta, umbilical cord and amniotic sac develop to maturity.
- All important external and internal features continue to develop. Baby's vocal cords begin to develop. The liver begins to secrete bile and the pancreas to produce insulin.
- All twenty baby teeth are formed and wait beneath his gums until well after birth. However, every once in a while a baby is born with teeth already showing.
- The heart has four chambers and beats at 120 to 160 beats per minute. Kidneys are now developed and start draining urine into the bladder. Intestines have formed outside of the baby (on the umbilical cord) because they cannot fit inside the baby.
- By the end of this month, the umbilical cord, which carries nutrients to your baby and takes wastes away, will be fully formed.
- At the end of third month, baby weighs just over 1 ounce and is about 4 inches long.

Ideal Weight Gain in First Trimester

In early pregnancy during the first trimester the weight gain does not take place, the weight of the pregnant lady should remain constant. In some cases the weight can even fall due to lack of appetite and morning sickness. The actual weight gain begins from the 10th week when the circulating blood volume begins to increase. In between 10 to 14 weeks, 1.5 kilograms is gained. Food intake of the lady also increases as nausea and vomiting decrease by the 14th week adding to weight gain.

Common Problems during First Trimester

1. Morning Sickness

Commonly known as nausea and vomiting, morning sickness is most likely one of the first pregnancy symptoms to be experienced. On an average at least 60% to 80% of all pregnant women experience this problem. Contrary to what the term may suggest, it does not always or only, occurs in the morning. An increase in morning sickness can be experienced at any time of the day. It starts somewhere between the fourth and sixth week of pregnancy and is, therefore, one of the first pregnancy signs. For most women, morning sickness disappears by the 14th to 16th week. Some women experience morning sickness throughout their pregnancy.

Causes of morning sickness

1. Excessive hormone production in early pregnancy disturbs the physiological and biochemical balances which lead to gastrointestinal disturbances.
2. Tensions, anxieties, mental and physical stress of the mother while dealing with changes in pregnancy.
3. Fad diets, poor nutrition, disturbed eating schedules are main causes of morning sickness.
4. Hypersensitivity to different smells during pregnancy is also a factor.

"I was so fed up of my morning sickness during the initial stages of pregnancy, that it started showing on my personality. I could not eat anything properly and began to dislike almost everything. I became temperamental and irritable and lost temper frequently. I did not know what to do as I understood this was a common problem during first trimester of pregnancy. I happened to chance upon this yoga and diet thing recommended by Nishtha and adopted it. I was actually surprised with the results that I got. I became calmer, the vomiting reduced considerably and I could tolerate more smells and food items now. I became more cheerful now and started enjoying my pregnancy!"

— Anju Chauhan, Simla

Yoga therapy for morning sickness

1. Micro Exercise for *Kapal* (Brain)

(Mentioned in Infertility and Inability to Conceive on page no. 46)

2. Ananda Madirasana

- Sit in Vajrasana.
- Place the palms on top of the heels so that the fingers are pointing towards each other, if this is uncomfortable place the palms just above the heels.
- Keep the spine erect and head tilted backwards, close the eyes and relax the whole body.
- Fix the attention at the *bhrumadhya* (the eyebrow centre).
- The physical awareness should be on eyebrow centre and spiritual awareness should be on *ajna chakra*.

Breathing: Breathe slowly and deeply. Imagine that the breath is moving in and out of the eyebrow centre. Inhale from the eyebrow centre to *ajna chakra* and exhale from *ajna chakra* to the eyebrow centre.

3. Padadirasana

- Sit in Vajrasana.
- Cross the arms in front of the chest, placing the hands under the opposite armpits with the thumbs pointing upward.

- The point between the thumb and first finger should be firmly pressed.
- Close the eyes and become aware of breathing process.
- Physical awareness should be on the breathing process in the nose and spiritual awareness should be on *ajna chakra.*

Breathing: Slow, and deep and rhythmical breathing is required. Practise until the flow of breath in both nostrils becomes equalised.

Duration: Practise for 5 to 10 minutes.

4. Shavasana

(Mentioned in Infertility and Inability to Conceive on page no. 43)

5. Ujjai Pranayama

- Sit in any comfortable posture preferably a meditation asana.
- Close the eyes and relax the whole body.
- Take the awareness to the breath in the nostrils and allow the breathing to become calm and rhythmic.
- After some time, transfer the awareness to the throat.
- Try to feel or to imagine that the breath is being drawn in and out through the throat and not through the nostrils, as if inhalation and exhalation are taking place through a small hole in the throat.
- As the breathing becomes slower and deeper, gently contract the glottis so that a soft snoring sound like the breath of the sleeping baby is produced in the throat.
- If this is practised correctly there will be a simultaneous contraction of the abdomen. This happens by itself, without any effort being made.
- Both inhalation and exaltation should be long, deep and controlled.
- Sound of breath should not be very loud. It should just be audible to the practitioner but not to another person unless they are sitting very close.

Repetition: Practise this for 10 to 20 minutes.

6. Anulom Vilom Pranayama

Sit in any comfortable cross-legged position with backbone straight. Control the flow of breath with thumb and ring finger of right hand by alternately pressing on the nostrils. Index, middle and little finger will remain relaxed and comfortably folded while performing pranayama.

- Close the right nostril with right thumb.
- Inhale through left nostril with complete awareness.
- Now close the left nostril with right ring finger and remove the thumb from right nostril.
- Now exhale through the right nostril.
- Similarly repeat the process by inhaling through right nostril and exhaling through the left.

- This completes one round. Make sure that there is no sound of air passing while performing this pranayama. Avoid forced breathing or rapid counts.

Repetition: Repeat the procedure 10 to 15 times.

Diet therapy for morning sickness

Feeling good about being pregnant is the key to get relief from morning sickness. Remember, this is a part of the process of pregnancy and is natural. Psychology of the mother plays a very important role in frequency and effects of morning sickness. Therefore strengthen your will-power and get ready to deal with morning sickness.

Make yourself busy — the more you think of the problem, the worse it can get. Wear clothes that are not too tight around the waist and chest. Get as much sleep and rest as you can. If you feel sick in the mornings, give yourself time and get up slowly.

Mild morning sickness can usually be overcome by the use of high carbohydrate foods like toast early in the morning. Fatty and rich foods, highly seasoned and flavoured foods may be restricted. Ample amounts of fluids, carbohydrates and water soluble vitamins should be added to the diet. If excessive, persistent and prolonged vomiting is seen, this is called *Hyperemesis Gravidarum.* This is a rare and severe form of morning sickness and may require hospitalisation to restore lost fluids and weight. Patient is fed intravenously to prevent complications and dehydration.

Dietary tips to overcome morning sickness

1. Early in the morning take suji rusk or a plain biscuit with milk or tea.
2. Apply small meal patterns to your diet during this period. Eat small amounts of food often rather than several large meals. So that your stomach is never empty. Taking liquids between meals give better results.
3. Avoid the foods and smells that make you feel bad.
4. Eating foods that contain ginger may be helpful. Researches have shown that ginger is an effective morning sickness remedy. Usually herbal supplements are not recommended for a pregnant woman, ginger is found to have no apparent side-effects. Ginger is easy to incorporate into your lifestyle. You can simply add ginger to your tea along with tulsi leaves.
5. Put tulsi leaves in your mouth, they will help reduce vomiting and improve taste.
6. Drink plenty of fluids throughout the day. Add lots of water; take fresh fruit juices mainly mixed fruit, small servings of cold milk after every two hours etc.
8. Eating raw amla or sucking lemon candies help in reducing the morning sickness.

2. Anaemia

Anaemia is a matter of real concern during pregnancy. It is common among 60% to 70% of pregnant ladies. Anaemia is a condition where haemoglobin levels in the blood fall below normal levels. As we know that the capacity of heart to pump the blood is increased by 33% during pregnancy, with this increase the concentration of plasma proteins, haemoglobin and other blood constituents are lowered. The normal haemoglobin level drops down resulting in anaemia. Some pregnant women have too little iron in their blood. Anaemia can occur because the foetus takes iron from the mother's bloodstream to make its own red blood cells. Anaemia can also occur due to deficiency in folic acid and vitamin B_{12}. Haemoglobin levels below 11g/100 ml are considered anaemic during pregnancy.

Anaemia is characterised by fatigue, giddiness, breathlessness, palpitation, loss of appetite, paleness or whiteness (in severe cases) of certain body parts. Some patients may feel a pricking sensation as somebody is pricking them with pins or needles on the fingers and toes.

Anaemia in pregnant women leads to premature delivery. They usually give birth to low-birth-weight babies. These women have greater risks of catching infections of uterus, kidneys and the urinary tract which creates bigger complications in pregnancy. Severe anaemia can even lead to death. The risk of death is higher in severely anaemic women particularly during delivery.

Yoga therapy for anaemia during pregnancy

1. Modified Hastapadasana

- Stand with spine erect, feet together and hands beside the body. Relax the body.
- Distribute the weight of the body evenly on both feet.
- Slowly bend forward, first bending the head, taking the chin towards the chest, then bending the upper trunk, relaxing the shoulders forward and letting the arms go limp.
- Bend the mid trunk and finally the lower trunk.
- While bending forward, imagine that the body has no bones or muscles. Do not strain or force the body.
- Place the fingers underneath the toes or bring the palms to the floor beside the feet. If this is not possible, bring the fingertips as near to the floor as possible.
- Relax the back of the neck and bend it loosely towards the knees.
- Do not try to touch the forehead to the knees.
- Hold the position, relaxing the whole back.
- Slowly return to the starting position in the reverse order.
- This completes one round.
- Relax in the upright position before continuing the next round.

Modified Hastapadasana

Repetition: Repeat 5 such rounds slowly and gradually. Practise one round for 3 to 5 minutes.

Breathing: Inhale in the starting position. Exhale while bending forward. Breathe slowly and deeply in the final position.

2. Matsyasana

(Mentioned in Infertility and Inability to Conceive on page no. 42)

3. Shavasana

(Mentioned in Infertility and Inability to Conceive on page no. 43)

4. Anulom Vilom Pranayama

(Mentioned in Yoga therapy for morning sickness'on page no. 64)

5. Seetkari Pranayama

- Sit in any comfortable meditation posture.
- Close the eyes and relax the body.
- Hold the teeth tightly together.
- Separate the lips, exposing the teeth.
- The tongue may be kept flat or folded against the soft palate.
- Breathe in slowly and deeply through the teeth making hissing sound.
- At the end of inhalation close the mouth, keeping the tongue either flat or folded.
- Breathe out slowly through the nose in a controlled manner.
- This is one round. Awareness should be on the hissing sound.

Seetkari Pranayama

Repetition: Practise 9 such rounds. Gradually increase the number of rounds from 10 to 15 and the duration of each inhalation and exhalation.

Diet therapy for anaemia during pregnancy

To keep your bloodstream flowing strongly and smoothly, certain dietary modifications are necessary to revitalise it. Anaemia is caused mainly due to inadequate diet. Let us learn how to eliminate this disease completely and easily during pregnancy with the help of certain modifications in our diet.

Dietary modifications

Proteins

Proteins are very important as they are one of the main constituents of the blood haemoglobin. Red blood cells contain more protein than iron. So, all essential amino acids should be provided by the diet. Take ample amount of proteins in the diet. Some good quality protein-rich foods are milk and milk products, eggs, wheat germ, yeast, pulses, especially soyabeans (you can also take soya milk) and legumes, green leafy vegetables, nuts and oilseeds. Milk is the only animal food which is used by the vegetarians, although the protein content in milk is only 3.2 grams yet it contains very good quality protein and is rich in essential amino acid Lysine. So milk should necessarily be added in the diet. The combination of protein-rich foods is of great help in treatment of anaemia.

Minerals

Minerals also play very important role in curing anaemia. Iron is the other big constituent of the haemoglobin. Green leafy vegetables like amaranth leaves, Bengal gram leaves (*Chana sag*) parsley, turnip greens, mustard leaves, colocasia leaves, mint leaves and some other vegetables like lotus stem, onion stalks are also very rich sources of iron. Lotus stem (*Kamal kakdi*), in particular has the highest content of iron i.e. 60.6 milligrams per 100 grams and onion stalks has 7.5 milligrams of iron per 100 grams edible portion, where as animal origin food lever has only 6.3 milligrams of iron per 100 grams. Milk product *khoya,* rice flakes, nuts and oil seeds like cashew nuts, almond, coconut dry, gingelly seeds (*Til*), niger seeds *(Kala til),* mustard seeds and some spices and condiments like cumin seeds, cloves, fenugreek seeds, mango powder, mace and asafoetida also contain good amount of iron. Add ample amounts of these foods in daily diet to overcome anaemia.

Vitamins

All the B complex group of vitamins are essential in the formation of healthy red blood cells. In particular, folic acid and vitamin B_{12} appear to be the causative factor of pernicious anaemia. Folic acid deficiency is seen most commonly in those pregnant women who consume diets that do not contain vegetables, fruits and milk regularly right through their lives. Folic acid is widely distributed in the nature foods. The good sources of folic acid are whole grain cereals, leafy vegetables, milk and all dairy products.

Other Nutrients

Other nutrients should be taken in the proper amounts as indicated in recommended dietary allowances.

Continue these modifications along with yoga therapy till normal blood count is attained. Even after achieving normal blood count, continue to follow these dietary guidelines in order to avoid recurrence of anaemia during pregnancy.

3. Frequent Urination

Frequent urination is a common and tiresome symptom experienced by all pregnant women. It starts at about six weeks into the first trimester and is worse during the first trimester and again towards the end of pregnancy. It is mostly because the amount of blood in the body increases dramatically during pregnancy, which leads to a lot of extra fluid getting processed through the kidneys and ending up in the bladder. Eventually, the pressure is felt on the bladder from growing uterus.

It tends to be more troublesome in succeeding pregnancies because of the increasing laxity of the muscles which support the bladder. You may notice that you need to get up more often during the night in particular to attend to the nature's call. That is because when you lie down, some of the fluid that you retained in your legs and feet during the day makes its way back into your bloodstream and eventually into your bladder.

There is unfortunately no cure but here are a few suggestions which may be helpful:

- Drink water only when you are thirsty and not for any other reason.
- Avoid beverages that have a mild diuretic effect, such as coffee and tea.
- Do not drink water at night if you want a full night's sleep.
- When you urinate, lean forward to help completely empty your bladder.
- If the frequency is accompanied by pain you should consult your doctor.

Yoga

Regular Yogic Workouts during First Trimester

These points should be considered before starting the practice of yoga during pregnancy:

- Never perform asanas during pregnancy similar to the normal daily yogic routine nor start all of a sudden. Prepare yourself physically and mentally before you begin with the practice of yoga during pregnancy.
- Wash yourself, clear your stomach, nose and throat, spread your mat on the floor and sit comfortably for at least ten minutes in crossed leg or folded knee position with spine straight and head relaxed.
- Suspend all worries for the time being and concentrate just on yourself.
- Let your mind be stress free, joints and muscles tension free, face should feel cool and calm and breathing should be rhythmic. This practice will suspend your worries and problems forever.
- Stop immediately if you feel any strain or discomfort, but at the same time do not be too easy on yourself. The baby is well protected both by your abdominal muscles and by its sac of amniotic fluid in the womb.
- Remember, the baby in the womb screams with fear when you are in fear, it flourishes when you bear a cheer. It gets proper nourishment when you are nourished. It is within

you, is a part of your existence and is directly affected by the changes that occur to your personality, so be very careful and balanced as you are shaping a new creation.

- While at yoga, devote yourself absolutely to the asanas and imagine the baby too moving with you while practising asana.
- Listen to your body as you are the best judge of what you can and cannot do while you are pregnant and how to adapt your asana to meet your own particular need.
- At the end, relaxation is a must for at least 10 minutes.

1. Dhruvasana

- Stand straight on your mat and grip your right ankle with left hand to rest your left sole on the right thigh. Keep the palms beside both thighs.
- Balance on the right leg and lift both arms from sides to above head position while inhaling. Give a moderate upward stretch to your entire body and bring the palms to observe prayer pose in front of your chest while exhaling.
- Continue to be in the prayer pose with rhythmic breathing. Keep balancing gradually with eyes closed for perfect results.
- Concentrate on breathing rhythm only to develop wonderful feeling of inner peace and concentration to steady the mind.
- Repeat it with changing the position of legs. The calming influence of the asana will be enormously rewarding during the months to come. Practise both positions – stretching and the prayer pose, placing your foot high against the opposite thigh. Try to hold the position with eyes closed.

Dhruvasana

Benefits: This asana may be performed even during late pregnancy and prevents any deformity. This asana adds a lot of muscular and nervous strength and energy and refreshes you against any fatigue. It protects you against painful labour. This asana strengthens your legs, helping to carry the baby comfortably. Women who practise this Dhruvasana during pregnancy are blessed with healthy baby with wonderful devotion and concentration like *Bhakta Dhruva.*

2. Padmasana

- Sit with legs spread in front of your body.
- Hold the right toe with your hands to rest the right ankle on left thigh joint. Now hold the left toe to rest the left ankle on right thigh joint.
- Ensure both heels touching the lower abdomen with your spine, neck and head quite straight but still tension free.
- Sit comfortably but try gradually to ensure that your both knees come closer to the floor. You may try on single leg also alternately in the beginning if you find it tough to perform all together.

- Hold *Brahmanjali Mudra* during Padmasana. Rest your palms in your lap below naval placing right palm over your left palm facing sky. It will equip you with *Laghima shakti* and keep you very light at body and mind during this tough period.
- You may prefer to sit in *Gyan Mudra* and if feel the necessity of *Garima shakti,* then with index finger of both hands make a circle while touching the tip of the thumb.
- Keep the complete arm relaxed, resting the wrists and knees.

Padmasana

Repetition: Close your eyes and try to remain seated in the posture for 5 to 10 minutes. If in starting you are not able to perform it for too long then repeat it 4 to 5 times for two minutes each time.

Benefits: Padmasana is popularly known as '*Sarva Vyadhi Vinashanam*' or the rare asana that eradicates all ailments from the body of its practitioner. This asana tones up your digestion generally disturbed during pregnancy and develops a rhythm and strength among stomach, heart and mind. Padmasana helps to open up the pelvis for the birth.

3. Gomukhasana

- Sit with your legs spread straight in front of your body.
- Fold the right knee, hold the right toe with left hand and bring your right heel closer to left side of buttocks.
- The same way fold the left knee holding the left toe with right hand and bring the left heel closer to right side of buttocks.
- Ensure that your knees are placed one over the other and your right knee is placed over the left one.
- Keep the spinal column straight and lift your right arm above your head allowing the upper arm touching the right ear.
- Fold it at elbow so that the palm touches your upper back.
- Now try to catch it with left hand from back side.
- Hold this position and continue deep rhythmic inhalation and exhalation for about 20 times.
- Ensure that the chest is lifted high and back is maintained straight during Gomukhasana.
- Try to hold the posture for 3 to 5 minutes each side.
- Repeat the same process with changed positions of knees and arms.

Gomukhasana

Benefits: It strengthens the legs, arms, knee and back. In the first trimester of pregnancy, muscle cramps is a common complaint. Gomukhasana helps in decreasing its rate and frequency. Gomukhasana is specially meant for people suffering from breathing problems especially asthma and bronchitis. Pregnant women facing breathlessness and short breathing with increasing size of baby in the womb are deeply benefited with regular practice of Gomukhasana. Ample oxygen supply in this asana purifies the lungs and adds proper purified blood supply to entire body and the growing baby and decrease the chances of anaemia. It helps activating the milk glands in women before the child takes birth. The cross-legged position in this particular asana supports the lower abdomen in a balanced way which is already bearing the weight of growing baby for over nine months.

4. Bhramri Pranayama
   (Mentioned in Infertility and Inability to Conceive on page no. 43)

5. Anulom Vilom Pranayama
   (Mentioned under 'Yoga therapy for morning sickness' on page no. 64)

Dietetics

Regular Diet during First Trimester

In the first trimester, the growth takes place only by an increase in the number of cells. Inadequate diet during this period of cell division can depress the cell number which cannot be made better by taking an adequate diet at a later date. The effect of malnutrition at this stage is permanent. Increase in the number of cells requires folic acid and vitamin B_{12}. Both these vitamins play an important role in the synthesis of nucleic acids, which must be produced each time a cell divides. During the early stages of pregnancy, the placenta is not formed yet, so there is no mechanism to protect the embryo from the deficiencies which may be inherent in the mother's circulation, so it is critical that the correct amount of nutrients are consumed during this period.

In the second phase of this trimester, the new cells continue to form and already formed ones continue to increase in size. This process is called hypertrophy. This phase particularly requires proteins and vitamin B_6.

Dietary modifications during first trimester

Vitamins

Proper vitamin intake during this part of pregnancy reduces the risk of birth defects of the brain and spinal cord (called neural tube defects). The most common neural tube defect is *spina bifida* (in which the vertebrae do not fuse together properly, causing the spinal cord to be exposed) which can lead to varying degrees of paralysis, incontinence, and sometimes mental retardation.

Let us have a look on the daily dietary intake and food sources of vitamins essential during this part of pregnancy.

- **Folic acid:** During the early stages of pregnancy, folic acid happens to be the most required nutrient to help rapid cell division and growth. The US Public Health Service and Indian Council of Medical Research (ICMR) recommends that all women of child-bearing age consume 400 micrograms (0.4 milligrams) of folic acid each day.

  Folic acid is most beneficial during the first 28 days after conception, when most neural tube defects occur. But it is very unfortunate that most of the women do not realise they are pregnant before 28 days. Therefore, folic acid intake should begin before conception from the time one is ready to conceive and should continue through pregnancy. The requirement of folic acid in the body varies from individual to individual depending upon their blood count and other personal features. Your physician will recommend the appropriate amount of folic acid to meet your individual needs. However, a prenatal supplement does not replace a healthy diet. Try to meet your nutritional needs with diet rather than taking supplements. Folic acid is widely distributed in nature foods. Excellent food sources are green leafy vegetables like amaranth, cabbage, most berries, nuts, tomato, whole grain cereals, milk and milk products, pulses especially Bengal gram, red gram, soyabeans, gingelly seeds, groundnut and coconut.
- **Vitamin B_{12}:** Vitamin B_{12} also plays an important role in cell division and their growth. According to Indian Council of Medical Research only 1 microgram is recommended per day for pregnancy. But during first trimester it should be increased to 1.5 micrograms per day. This vitamin is entirely derived from animal foods. Good sources of this vitamin are milk and milk products mainly in whole milk, curd and skimmed milk powder, fish, eggs and organ meats especially liver of sheep and goat.
- **Vitamin B_6 or Pyridoxine:** This vitamin is important in the second phase of this trimester along with proteins. Vitamin B_6 plays an important role in the protein metabolism and in the metabolism of essential fatty acids. The recommended daily intake of this vitamin during this trimester is 2.5 milligrams. The food sources of pyridoxine are vegetables, whole grain cereals like jowar, rice, wheat whole, red gram, skimmed milk powder, whole milk powder and *khoya*. This vitamin has limited food sources, therefore, make sure to add these products in your daily diet.
- **Other vitamins:** Other vitamins should also be taken in adequate amounts according to the recommended dietary allowances for pregnant woman prescribed by Indian Council of Medical Research.

Minerals

- **Calcium:** Calcium is used by every cell in the body. That is why its intake becomes very important in the first trimester. In this trimester, the skeleton also begins to form which requires calcium in sufficient amounts. Not only does calcium help keep bones and teeth strong and healthy, it also helps keep the circulatory, muscular and nervous systems running normally. When a pregnant woman does not get enough calcium from her diet to meet the requirements of her foetus, the body takes calcium from her bones to maintain steady levels in the blood and to nourish the foetus. Over the time, this loss may significantly weaken her bones and lead to osteoporosis. The daily recommended dietary intake of calcium suggested by ICMR is 1000 milligrams or 1 gram of calcium per day. This daily intake of calcium takes care of total calcium needs of the mother and the additional needs of the foetus.

Some excellent sources of calcium are milk and milk products like curd, *khoya*, cottage cheese. Among nuts and oilseeds, gingelly seeds in particular are excellent source of calcium. Others like coconut, almonds and walnuts and pulses like bengal gram, black gram, green gram, moth beans, kidney beans, soyabeans, green leafy vegetables like amaranth leaves, colocasia leaves, fenugreek leaves have mustard leaves have fairly good amount of calcium. Cereals too are rich sources of calcium.

- **Iron:** Iron is one of the main constituents of blood and during the first phase of pregnancy the nourishment to the embryo is supplied from mother's blood only. Daily requirement of iron during this trimester according to ICMR is 38 milligrams per day. The food sources of iron include whole pulses; soya bean is exceptionally good source of iron; cereals like whole wheat flour, rice flakes, bajra, ragi, jowar; green leafy vegetables like mustard leaves, mint leaves, colocasia leaves, amaranth leaves; jaggery also contains fair amounts of iron.
- **Other minerals:** Other minerals are also important and should be taken according the recommended dietary allowances suggested by ICMR.

Protein

In the first trimester, additional proteins are necessary for the formation of amniotic fluid, development of the placenta, increased volume of mother's blood and for the growth of foetus. The daily recommended intake of protein for a pregnant woman is 65 grams per day. The rich food sources of proteins are milk and milk products, eggs, wheat germ, yeast, pulses especially soyabeans (you can also take soya milk) and legumes, green leafy vegetables, nuts and oilseeds.

Energy

Increase in the daily requirement of energy is not recommended in the first trimester. At this stage, energy demands are not too much because the foetus is still growing and much weight gain does not take place. But this does not means that energy intake is not important in this trimester; adequate energy intake is as important as the intake of proteins and other nutrients. Energy during this trimester is needed for development of placenta, growth of foetus and also in development of maternal tissues.

The daily recommended requirement of energy for this trimester for moderate working women is 2225 kilocalories per day. The best sources of energy are all cereal grains as they contain 60% to 70% of energy in them. Among cereals, rice, wheat, bajra, ragi, jowar are exceptionally rich in energy content, pulses also contain good amounts of energy especially soyabeans, kidney beans, cowpea, green gram, bengal gram, black gram, nuts and oilseeds like almond, cashewnut, chilgoza, dry and fresh coconut, pistachio, gingelly seeds, mustard seeds are concentrated form of energy. Among fruits banana, dates, black current, dry apricot etc are rich in energy. Besides, roots and tubers, milk and milk products, especially cottage cheese, all fats and edible oils, and all sugars are rich sources of energy.

Other Nutrients

All other nutrients should be taken as recommended by Indian Council of Medical Research (ICMR).

Special menu plan

MEAL	TIME	MENU		
		Exchange 1	*Exchange 2*	*Exchange 3*
Early Morning	6.30 am	Lemon tea, cookies of your choice	Tea, cake rusks	Tea, biscuits
Before Breakfast	8.00 am	Lemon and honey mixed water	Lemon and honey mixed water	Lemon and honey mixed water
Breakfast	9.00 am	Broken wheat porridge (*dalia*) in milk (add some dry fruits to it), besan chilla, 1 medium sized apple	Suji (rawa) porridge in milk (add some dry fruits to it), wheat bread with omelette/cheese sandwich (wheat bread), 1 banana	Idli/Vada with sambhar and coconut chutney, buttermilk, 1 guava/orange
After Breakfast	10.30 am	Fresh mix fruit juice	Fresh carrot, amla, beetroot juice	Fresh apple or tomato juice
Mid-morning	11.30 am	Vegetable idli	Sprout chat	Khaman dhokla
Lunch	1.00 pm	Tomato spinach soup, soyabean potato curry, red gram dal (*tuar dal*), rice, mix vegetable, chapattis, bottle gourd raita, mint chutney, salad and jaggery (*gur*)	Rasam, masala dosa/mix veg uttapam, sambar, curd rice, coconut chutney and jaggery (*gur*) after meal	Sweet corn soup, chana curry, potato peas vegetable, methi puri, curd, mint raita, salad of sprouts and jaggery (*gur*)
After lunch	3.30 pm	Kaju barfi	Besan laddoo	Til-jaggery

MEAL	TIME	MENU		
		Exchange 1	*Exchange 2*	*Exchange 3*
Evening Snack	5.15 pm	Banana milkshake, roasted cashew and groundnut along with pistachio and walnuts, 1 snack of your choice	Strawberry milkshake, potato poha with roasted peanuts	Laddoo Ginger-tulsi leaves tea, mix vegetable pakoras/mix fruit chat/sweet potato, lotus stem chaat
Dinner	8.15 pm	Methi mutter (peas) malai vegetable, mix veg pulao, kidney beans curry, curd, salad of sprouts, onion parantha Til-gur laddoo as dessert	Cabbage peas potato vegetable, cow pea curry, boondi raita, vegetable biryani, chapatti, green salad Fruit cream as dessert	Spinach mustard leaves saag, makka roti, Bengal gram dal, rice, curd, salad, fruit. Custard as dessert
Bedtime	11.00 pm	Hot almond milk	Hot almond milk	Hot almond milk

Precautions to be taken during First Trimester

Pregnancy is a very sensitive period for both the mother and the little one growing in the womb. The safety of the child depends entirely upon the safety measures taken by the mother to be. Therefore, the mother has to take several precautions throughout the pregnancy. The first trimester of pregnancy is the most significant since this is the period where initial development from cells to embryo to foetus takes place and all organs begin to take shape and start functioning. Here are some directions about the precautions to be taken during this trimester:

- Do not eat raw, uncooked or undercooked meat and eggs. Eat cooked meals only.
- Do not overcook vegetables, as it leads to loss of nutrients.
- Do not eat raw vegetables either and also wash all the fruits nicely before consuming.
- Avoid taking caffeinated beverages like coffee, tea, colas because excessive intake of caffeine may result in caffeine entering the foetal circulation developing the risk of miscarriage, several abnormalities and the development of diabetes later in life. There are several other reasons to cut down the intake of caffeine; drinking coffee and tea spoils appetite and can affect normal sleep pattern, creates insomnia and aggravates mood swings. Caffeine may also interfere with the absorption of some essential nutrients.

- If you are a non-vegetarian and love eating fish and seafood then keep a tight hand on their consumption amount because although fish and seafood are excellent low-fat sources of many nutrients but mercury is a contaminant found in fish that can affect brain development and the nervous system of the foetus. There is a concern about eating fish and seafood during pregnancy, since many types of fishes may contain high levels of mercury. Eat no more than 12 ounces of cooked fish a week. Do not eat sharks, swordfish, king mackerel or tilefish.
- While planning a day's menu for yourself add foods from each food group, because all food groups are important in the quest of adding all essential nutrients in your diet.
- Do not try to do any other vigorous exercises other than yoga therapy prescribed here in this book and do not try to mould them according to your liking. Perform yoga therapy step by step and in the same sequence as mentioned in the book. Stop all exercises in case you notice any sign of persistent discomfort or pain and consult your doctor.
- Consult your doctor before taking any medication or drugs without doctor's advice.
- Consult your doctor immediately if nausea, diarrhoea, or vomiting persists severely for longer than 24 hours.
- Beware of toxic chemicals like pesticides.
- Avoid alcohol and smoking and also don't allow anybody to smoke near you.
- Avoid stress, create a positive environment full of laughter. Indulge in good books, greenery and soothing music to keep your mind occupied and tension free.
- Avoid jerks, accidents and always wear a seatbelt while travelling in a car.

The Second Trimester

The second trimester covers the next three months i.e. fourth, fifth and sixth months of pregnancy. This is the most beautiful and enjoyable period of pregnancy because you start feeling your baby by this trimester. A special bonding starts developing between the mother and the child. By the onset of second trimester you start feeling more energetic and fresh as morning sickness subsides and the risk of miscarriage drops now. Your tummy starts increasing in size.

Foetal Development in Second Trimester

Foetal Development by the End of Fourth Month

- The baby's skin is pink and somewhat transparent. Blood vessels are still visible. It is covered by a fine, soft layer of hair called lanugo. This layer helps to insulate your baby.
- Eyebrows and eyelashes begin to appear in this month. Buds on the side of the head begin to form into the outer ear.
- The baby's face continues to develop. The tail disappears from the foetus and the head makes up about half of the baby's size.
- The baby's neck is long enough to lift the head from the body.
- The baby moves, kicks, sleeps, wakes, swallows, and passes urine.
- You may start to feel a slight sensation in your lower abdomen (called quickening). This feels like bubbles or fluttering. When you feel the baby's movement, write down the date and tell your doctor. This helps determine when your baby is due.
- The baby can probably hear now and is comforted by the sound of your heartbeat and your voice.
- By the end of the fourth month, baby is 8 to 10 inches long and weighs about 6 ounces.

Foetal Development by the End of Fifth Month

- This is a period of tremendous growth for the baby. The internal organs start maturing.
- The baby's fingernails grow to the tips of the fingers. Fat is now being stored beneath the baby's skin.
- The baby is also growing muscle and is getting stronger every day.
- The baby's gall bladder becomes functional, producing bile necessary for digestion.

- The baby's first bowel movement called Meconium is beginning to accumulate in the bowel. It is made up of undigested debris from the amniotic fluid and various secretions of the digestive tract.
- Tiny air sacs called alveoli begin to form in lungs.
- Vocal chords of the foetus are formed, though it is not possible for the baby to make sound in absence of air.
- Body hair, including eyebrows and eyelashes, start to grow.
- The baby sleeps and wakes at regular intervals. She is much more active now. She turns from side to side and head over heels. The baby may suck her thumb.
- At the end of the fifth month, baby will be about 10-12 inches long and will weigh about 1 pound.

Foetal Development by the End of Sixth Month

- By the end of this trimester the baby starts responding to your touch through your belly wall. Therefore touching and playing with the baby is possible now.
- The spine gets stronger and suppler to support the growing body of the foetus. It is now made up of 150 joints, 33 rings, and some 1,000 ligaments.
- The skin develops fast and becomes less transparent.
- Retinas begin to form and her optic nerve starts working. If an intense light is shown on the abdomen of the mother, in response to it the baby turn her head.
- The baby's brain develops rapidly. Fatty sheaths which transmit electrical impulses along nerves are forming.
- A special type of fat (brown fat) that keeps your baby warm at birth is forming.
- Baby girls develop eggs in their ovaries during this month.
- The baby's bones become solid.
- Your baby is almost fully formed and looks like a miniature human. However, because the lungs are not well-developed and the baby is still very small, a baby cannot usually live outside the uterus at this stage without highly specialised care.
- By the end of the sixth month, the baby is around 11 to 14 inches long and weighs about one and a half pounds.

Weight Gain in Second Trimester

This trimester witnesses the maximum weight gain. It is important to gain weight during this time to nourish the developing foetus and to store up reserves for breastfeeding. The ideal weight gain for the second trimester is 12 to 14 pounds in three months. The ideal weight gain between 14-20 weeks is 4-6 pounds or 2.5 kilograms and between 20-30 weeks is 10-12 pounds or 4.5 kilograms. So keep a close check on your weight during this trimester.

- **Excessive weight gain:** If there is a sudden weight gain of more than two pounds, accompanied by swelling of hands and face accompanied with headache or visual disturbances, you should call your doctor immediately.
- **Low weight gain:** Low weight gain during pregnancy (especially in second trimester) is not a good sign. It could indicate one of two complications: intrauterine growth retardation or oligohydramnios (less amniotic fluid around the foetus). Both of these conditions are related in the sense that oligohydramnios could be the cause for intrauterine growth retardation, or vice-versa. If the intrauterine growth retardation is a result of poor nutrition, it is important that the mother gets optimum nutrition and plenty of rest. If there is no weight gain for two consecutive weeks, you should consult your doctor.

Common Complications during Second Trimester

1. Heartburn or Gastric Troubles

Many women experience 'feeling of fullness' or heartburn during second trimester. Though it is generally harmless, it can be quite uncomfortable. This complaint or discomfort is generally felt after meals.

Heartburn is also called acid indigestion. This is a burning sensation that often extends from the bottom of the breastbone to the lower part of the throat. Food mixtures may sometimes be pushed back into the lower oesophagus. It is caused by some of the hormonal and gastrointestinal changes in the body of the mother. Pregnant women may also get heartburn because the stomach muscles relax and food tends to back up. Sometimes the stomach makes more acid during pregnancy. The growing baby pressing against the stomach can force acid upward, causing heartburn.

During pregnancy, the placenta produces the hormone progesterone, which relaxes the smooth muscles of the uterus. This hormone also relaxes the valve that separates the oesophagus from the stomach, allowing gastric acids to seep back up, which causes that unpleasant burning sensation.

Diet therapy for heartburn

It is not possible to eliminate heartburn during pregnancy entirely, but we can minimise the discomfort by taking few dietary measures:

- Avoid food and beverages that cause gastrointestinal distress, especially alcohol (which you should avoid anyway during pregnancy), caffeine, chocolate, acidic foods like citrus fruits and juices, tomatoes, mustard, and vinegar, processed meats, mint products, and spicy, highly seasoned, fried, or fatty foods.
- Try sipping water, milk, carbonated water to help coat your stomach and oesophagus. Eat 1/2 tablespoon of yogurt or heavy cream, or a small serving of vanilla ice cream when you feel the heartburn sensation. Drink plenty of liquids, especially water; but avoid drinking large quantities of fluids during meals.

- Avoid eating big meals. Instead, eat several small meals throughout the day. Take your time eating, and chew thoroughly.
- Take a chewing gum after eating. Chewing gum stimulates the salivary glands, and saliva can help neutralise acid.
- Do not eat close to bedtime. Give yourself two to three hours to digest before you lie down.
- While preparing to sleep, prop your upper body up with pillows and cushions. Elevating your upper body will help keep your stomach acids from upward movement and will aid your digestion.
- Avoid any tightness around your waist and tummy.
- Do not smoke — in addition to contributing to a host of serious health problems, smoking boosts stomach acidity.

Yoga therapy for heartburn

1. Ashwatthasana (traffic police posture)

- Stand straight on your yoga mat.
- Pull your left arm up while inhaling and spread the right arm to right side at shoulder level.
- Hold the breath and stretch the left leg as back as possible, try to lift it keeping maximum straight at knee and balance yourself.
- Hold your breath keeping the left arm pulled towards sky and right arm towards right side with chest lifted up.
- Come back to starting position while exhaling gently.
- Repeat it on other side also. It is one round of Ashwatthasana. Take at least 5 rounds.

Ashwatthasana

- Ashwatthasana is named after Peepal tree which is called Ashwatth in Sanskrit language. This is the only tree that gives oxygen round the clock. Our widely spread legs, arms and lifted chest represent the widely spread branches of Peepal tree.

Benefits: All the *Dasha Vayu* (Prana, Apana, Saman, Vyan, Udan, Naag, Kurma, Krikal, Devdutt, and Dhananjay) get a proper flow in our body and maximum oxygen is inhaled during the practice of this asana.

2. Hastothanasana

- Stand straight on your yoga mat.
- Put your hands downwards near to your thighs so that your palms touch the sides of the thighs.
- Now raise your arms quickly while inhaling, bringing the back of your hands together over your head.

- Without a pause lower your arms quickly while exhaling.

Repetition: Repeat 10 times. This was one round. Perform 5 such rounds.

3. Supta Padmasana

- Sit with legs spread in front of your body.
- Hold the right toe with your hands to rest the right ankle on left thigh joint. Now hold the left toe to rest the left ankle on right thigh joint.
- Ensure both heels touching the lower abdomen with your spine, neck and head quite straight but still tense free. This is Padmasana.
- Now slowly bend back, taking the support of first the right elbow and arm and then the left.
- Bring head and back to the ground.
- As you lie down on your back, the Padmasana position should be simultaneously raised so that the original position of Padmasana is maintained while lying down.
- Care should be taken not to strain the muscles and ligaments of the thighs and knees by forcing the knees to touch the ground in the final position.
- Close the eyes and relax the body.
- Breathe deeply and slowly in the final position.
- Return to the starting position in the reverse order, breathing in and taking support of the elbows and arms.
- Never leave the final position by straightening the legs first, this may dislocate the knee joint.
- Return to Padmasana first, then straighten the legs.

4. Singhasana

(Mentioned in Infertility and Inability to Conceive on page no. 47)

5. Seetkari Pranayama

(Mentioned in The First Trimester on page no. 67)

2. Hypertension

Hypertension is the technical term used for a condition of the body in which blood pressure is higher than normal. During pregnancy, hypertension may occur which may be mild or severe. (The normal blood pressure is 120 mm Hg/80 mm Hg.)

Pregnancy-induced hypertension

Pregnancy-induced hypertension, formally called toxemia is a combination of symptoms which include hypertension, oedema and albuminuria (increased protein 'albumin' in urine). It is a term applied to **pre-eclampsia** which is defined as appearance of swelling on the face and hands and albuminuria usually after the 20th week of the pregnancy. It usually takes place when there is a sudden weight gain and this weight gain is due to fluid retention rather than due to tissue building. It can affect the mother's kidney, liver, and brain and is also a leading cause of foetal complications, which include low birth weight, premature birth, and stillbirth.

Hypertension during pregnancy is of two types — mild pregnancy-induced hypertension and severe pregnancy-induced hypertension.

1. Mild pregnancy-induced hypertension

In this type of hypertension, the blood pressure is slightly raised, i.e. 140/90 mm Hg. There may be slight oedema of ankles and traces of albumin in the urine. The condition is quite common and is not of grave concern.

2. Severe pregnancy-induced hypertension

In severe case, the blood pressure is over 160/100 mm Hg. There is excessive oedema which extends to hands, face and abdomen. Albuminuria is severe. Symptoms are headache, disturbances of vision, vomiting and oliguria (lower volume of urine).

> *"I never knew that following a simple routine of yoga and diet can help so much. I never believed till I tried it myself. I was in my fourth month of pregnancy and had started experiencing things like high BP, swelling on face, arms, legs etc. I was worried as I had not seen anything like this earlier in my life. Someone suggested that I try yoga. I reluctantly agreed and started on my yoga and diet routine. And amazingly I got so much relief within a week that it was unbelievable!"*
>
> — Rakhi Kumar, Mumbai

Yoga therapy for pregnancy-induced hypertension

1. Standing Sarpasana

- Stand straight with feet together and palms on the thighs.
- Take your hands backward to support your back with them.
- While inhaling, bend your head and back backward as in Sarpasana. Hold the breath.
- Close your eyes and stay in the position as long as you can hold the breath.
- This is the final position.
- Exhale and bring your head and back to the starting position.
- Now bring your hands back on the thighs.
- Open your feet to your shoulder width and relax for a few seconds before repetition.

Repetition: Repeat 5 to 8 times.

Standing Sarpasana

2. Modified Hastapadasana

   (Mentioned in The First Trimester on pave no. 66)

3. Ananda Madirasana

   (Mentioned in The First Trimester on pave no. 63)

4. Padadirasana

   (Mentioned in The First Trimester on pave no. 63)

5. Gomukhasana

   (Mentioned in The First Trimester on pave no. 71)

6. Shavasana

   (Mentioned in Infertility and Inability to Conceive on page no. 43)

Meditation

- Select any of the meditative postures preferably Padmasana and practise meditation every day. (In case you are not able to sit on floor in Padmasana, you can do the same sitting straight in a chair).
- Begin with 10 minutes and increase time gradually every day till you attain perfection in at least one hour painless, comfortable and undisturbed sitting.
- Sit comfortably closing your eyes gently.
- Simply watch your breath with inner-self, incoming as well as outgoing. After five minutes of practice, recite any shortest possible mantra of your choice with flow of breath.
- It may best be holy OM. Feel the breath going inand out in the form of OM.
- Complete length of breath must be covered with flow of OM. Begin mental chanting of OM like this : 'O'... as you start inhaling and conclude inhaling with 'M'. Even while exhaling, begin with same 'O'... and conclude with same 'M'. See that there is no discontinuation in breath or in chanting of holy mantra 'OM'.
- You may come out of meditation with vocal chanting of same mantra three times.

Diet therapy for pregnancy-induced hypertension

In treatment of all cases of hypertension, diet plays a central role. In fact mild hypertension is controlled by dietary modifications only. While severe cases may require hospitalisation or complete bed rest, restriction on protein intake according to renal function, administration of diuretics to reduce oedema and restricted salt intake.

Dietary modifications

The fat-controlled sodium-restricted diet is prescribed for hypertension patients. It has been proved by the researches that intake of sodium directly influences blood pressure. It has also been found that restriction of sodium intake accompanied by fat restriction can effectively control hypertension.

In mild hypertension, just restriction of intake of common salt can be helpful. For severe hypertension patients, no salt is recommended to be used for cooking along with restriction of intake of the food stuffs rich in sodium. Food stuffs rich in sodium are baking powder or baking soda, preservatives, egg white, meat, fish, radish, carrot, lotus stem (dry) and pulses, therefore their intake should be restricted.

Reduce the intake of fats and oils. Use roasting, baking, boiling and steaming as methods of cooking. Use low-fat milk or toned milk instead of whole milk. Whole milk can be consumed after removing the fat or cream (*'malai'* which comes on the top after boiling). Increase the intake of fruits and vegetables especially fibrous ones because vitamins and minerals are regulatory agents which are particularly needed to avoid the general state of malnutrition which precedes toxemia.

3. Constipation

Constipation means hardening of stools, thereby resulting in difficult evacuation of the intestinal contents. This results in abnormal evacuation of body wastes and lazy elimination.

Constipation is a common complication among mothers during the later half of the pregnancy. This complication affects approximately 70% of pregnant women. Luckily, this is a minor complaint of the pregnancy and can be prevented thoroughly with yoga therapy and some modifications in the diet.

The main cause of constipation during pregnancy is hormonal change which tends to increase relaxation of intestinal walls, and causes food to stay longer in the digestive tract. The pressure of the enlarging uterus on the lower portion of the intestine also causes difficulty during elimination. Limited activity and exercise, insufficient fluid intake, insufficient bulk in diet are also important factors responsible for constipation.

Yoga therapy for constipation

1. Mrinalasana (the swaying lotus pose)
   - Stand with feet apart.
   - Fix the gaze of the point directly in the front.
   - Join your hands together in the prayer pose.
   - Inhale and raise the arms over the head.
   - While exhaling, bend to the left side from the waist.

Mrinalasana

- Do not bend forward or backward or twist the trunk.
- Hold the position for a few seconds while retaining the breath outside.
- Inhale and slowly come to the upright position.
- Repeat on the right side.
- From the upright position, exhale while bringing the arms down to the sides.
- This completes one round.

Repetition: Practise 10 to 15 rounds.

2. Skandhasana

- Stand with feet apart and palms on the thighs.
- Fix a gaze of point directly in the front.
- Raise the arms straight and bring them in front of chest.
- Now while inhaling twist the trunk to the extreme left taking your hands in the same direction.
- Retain breath and hold the position for few seconds.
- While exhaling come back to the starting position and repeat the same with right side.
- This is one round.

Skandhasana

Repetition: Practise 5 to 10 such rounds.

3. Shankhasana

- Sit in squatting position with the feet apart and the hands on the knees.
- Breathe in deeply, then breathe out, bringing the right knee to the floor near the left foot.
- Using the left hand as a lever, push the left knee towards the right, simultaneously twisting to the left.
- Keep the inside of the right foot on the floor.
- Look over the left shoulder. (Do not put extra pressure on your abdomen. If you feel the posture uneasy, leave the posture at once.)
- Hold the breath out for 3 to 5 seconds in the final position.
- Breathe in when returning to the starting position.
- Repeat on the other side of the body to complete one round.

Shankhasana

Repetition: Practise 5 rounds.

4. Vajrasana

Vajrasana

- Kneel on the floor.
- Bring the toes together and separate the heels.
- Lower the buttocks onto the inside surface of the feet with the heels touching the sides of the hips.
- Place hands on the knees with palms down.
- The back and head should be straight but not tense.
- Avoid excessive back arching of the spine.
- Close the eyes, relax the arms and the whole body.
- Breathe normally and fix the attention on the flow of air passing in and out of the nostrils.

Note: Practise Vajrasana as much as possible, especially directly after meals. Sit in Vajrasana for as long as possible and gradually increase the timing to at least 10 minutes to enhance the digestive function. Remember Vajrasana is the only asana in the yoga which can be practised after meals. Do not practise any other asana after meals.

Diet therapy for constipation

In the treatment of constipation, requirements of various nutrients are not altered, only few modifications in fibre, vitamin B complex, fats and fluid intake are suggested.

Dietary modifications

Fibre

The term fibre refers to a number of indigestible carbohydrates, like cellulose, present in plant foods. Research shows that though these indigestible components are not available to the body, yet they play an important role in the regulation of some body processes. Most important among them is elimination of the waste products from the body. Fibre helps in easy elimination of unabsorbed food in the form of stools or faeces from the body. Fibre present in stools holds water, makes them softer and hence helps in easy elimination. This particular function of fibre makes it useful for preventing or relieving constipation.

High fibre foods are whole grain cereals, whole pulses, green leafy vegetables and other fibrous vegetables and fruits like lotus stem, beans, peas, lady's fingers, guava, oranges and amla.

Fats

Foods containing fats are useful for some because of their lubricating effect and stimulating action of the fatty acids on the mucous membrane. Fat-rich foods are butter, ghee, cream, oils etc.

Fluids

Plenty of fluids are advised to the pregnant women suffering from constipation as it helps to soften the stools. A glass of warm water with lemon and 1 teaspoon of honey should be taken early in the morning to prevent constipation. An intake of 8 to 10 glasses of water is recommended along with a large amount of fluids in the form of soups, juices and other beverages. Avoid tea and coffee.

B vitamins

Ample supplies of B vitamins help in almost every case of lazy elimination. Add wheat germ ('*dalia*' the broken wheat grains), buttermilk, curd, eggs, nuts and oilseeds in your diet to get rid of constipation.

4. Leg Cramps

Leg cramps is a common discomfort associated with pregnancy. Although a cramp lasts for less than a minute, the pain can be very acute and intense and often unbearable. Leg cramps during pregnancy are a result of expanding uterus, as the uterus expands with the foetal growth it puts more pressure on the nerves and veins that send blood to and fro from the heart to the legs. Excess weight gain during pregnancy is another factor responsible for leg cramps. As the baby and the tummy of the mother grow bigger, the pressure of holding up and carrying the baby around is felt most by the legs.

Research shows that an excess of phosphorous could also cause leg cramps. This is because phosphorous hampers the body's ability to absorb calcium. Although a certain amount of phosphorous is good, too much can lead to leg cramps. Leg cramps can be prevented by keeping a close check on your weight and doing few yogic workouts daily.

Yoga therapy for leg cramps

Position: All modified yogic activities for leg cramps should be performed in the following position.

- Sit with legs outstretched.
- Place the palms of the hands on the floor to the sides and just behind the buttocks.
- The back, neck and head should be straight.
- Straighten the elbows.
- Lean back slightly, taking the support of arms.
- Close the eyes and relax the whole body in this position.

Activity 1: Toe bending

- Sit in the position as mentioned above with the legs outstretched and feet slightly apart.
- Place the hands beside and slightly behind the buttocks.

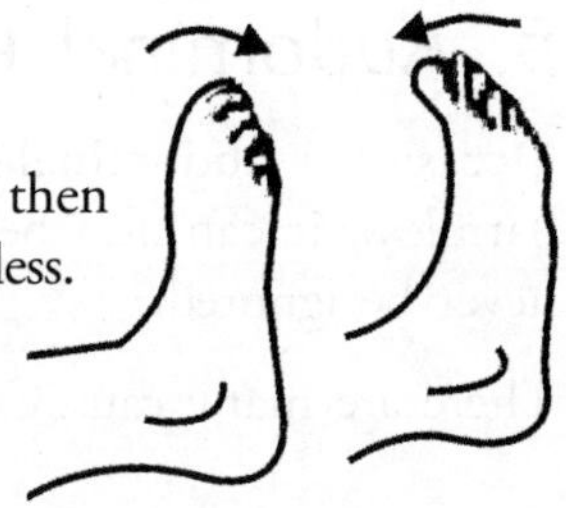

- Lean back a little using the arms to support the back.
- Keep the spine as straight as possible.
- Be aware of the toes, move the toes of feet slowly backward and then forward. Keeping the feet upright and the ankles relaxed and motionless.
- Hold each position for a few seconds.

Repetition: Repeat 10 to 15 times.

Breathing: Inhale as the toe move backward and exhale as the toes move forward. Keep the awareness on the stretching sensation produced by the movement.

Activity 2: Ankle bending

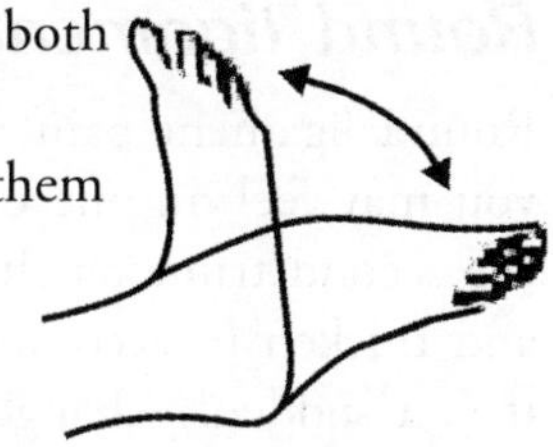

- Remain in the position. Keep the feet slightly apart. Slowly move both feet backwards and forward, bending them from the ankle joints.
- Try to stretch the feet forward to touch the floor and then draw them back towards the knees.
- Hold each position for few seconds.

Repetition: Repeat 10 to 15 times.

Breathing: Inhale as the feet move backward and exhale as the feet move forward. Keep the awareness on the stretching sensation in the foot, ankle, calf and leg muscles.

Activity 3: Ankle rotation

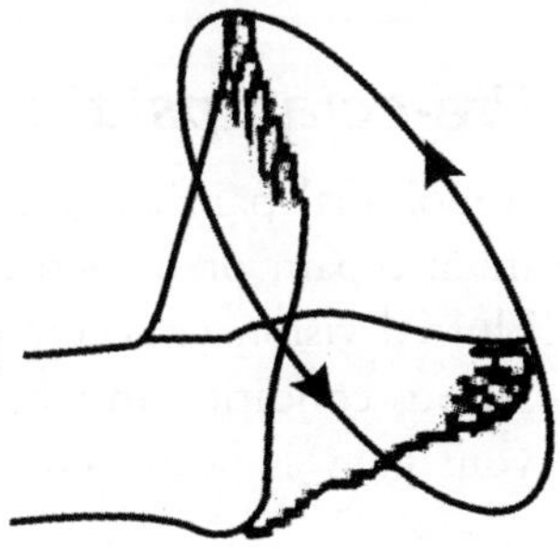

- Remain in the position.
- Separate the legs a little, keeping them straight.
- Keep the heels on the ground throughout the practice.
- Slowly rotate the right foot clockwise from the ankle 10 times and then repeat 10 times anti-clockwise.

Repetition: Repeat the same procedure with the left foot.

Breathing: Inhale on the upward movement and exhale on the downward movement.

Activity 4: Knee bending

- For this activity, lie down on your back on your yoga mat with your legs straight and one foot apart and hands straight with palms touching the floor on both sides of the hips.
- Lift your right leg gently from the floor and pull the heel as close to the right buttock as possible by bending at the knee.
- Now straighten the right leg but do not allow the heel to touch the floor.
- This is one round. Practise 10 such rounds with right leg and then repeat the same with left leg.

5. Abdominal Pain

Occasional abdominal discomfort is a common pregnancy complaint, and while it may be harmless, it can also be a sign of a serious problem. Severe or persistent abdominal pain should never be ignored.

There are many causes of abdominal discomfort or pain during pregnancy.

Gas and bloating

Gas pain and bloating during pregnancy is common because of hormones that slow the digestion and the pressure of the growing uterus on the stomach and intestines.

Round ligament pain

Round ligament pain is generally a brief, sharp, stabbing pain or a longer-lasting, dull ache that you may feel on one or both sides of the lower abdomen or deep in the groin, usually starting in the second trimester. It happens when the ligaments that support the uterus in your pelvis stretch and thicken to accommodate and support its growing size. You may feel a short jabbing sensation if you suddenly change position, such as when you are getting out of bed or up from a chair or when you cough, roll over in bed, or get out of the bathtub. Or you may feel a dull ache after a particularly active day, if you have been walking a lot or doing some other physical activity. Rest and deep rhythmic abdominal breathing is the best remedy for this condition. In case the problem persists even after sufficient rest, you should consult your doctor.

Pre-eclampsia

Abdominal pain could also be a result of pre-eclampsia. With severe pre-eclampsia, you may have intense pain or tenderness in the upper abdomen, a severe headache, visual disturbances (such as blurred vision or seeing spots), nausea and vomiting, placental abruption (placental abruption is a serious condition in which your placenta separates from your uterus, partially or completely, before your baby is born), etc.

If you experience abdominal pain or cramping along with spotting, bleeding, fever, chills, vaginal discharge, faintness, discomfort while urinating, or nausea and vomiting, or if the pain does not subside after several minutes of rest, then call your doctor.

Yoga

Regular Yogic Workouts during Second Trimester

1. Modified Tadasana

- Stand with feet together, body weight equally distributed on both legs and fingers interlocked in front of your chest with palms towards the ground.

- Pull your arms forward while inhaling through nostrils turning your palms to front and then lifting overhead with palms facing the sky.
- Hold the inhaled position as long as you can with complete body stretched upwards.
- Feel your ankles, calves, knee joints, thighs, pelvis, buttocks, trunk, chest, shoulders and arms perfectly stretched but do not pull them upwards.
- Lower the heels and bring the hands beside your thighs while exhaling gently.
- Relax perfectly with feet shoulder wide.

Repetition: Repeat the above mentioned steps 5 to 10 times.

Benefits: Tadasana is known for developing mental and physical balance. The entire spine is stretched and loosened, helping to clear up congestion of the spinal nerves at the points where they emerge from the spinal column. Tadasana stretches the abdominal muscles of rectum and intestines and is very useful in the first six months of the pregnancy to keep the abdominal muscles and nerves toned.

2. Mrinalasana

(Mentioned in Yoga therapy for constipation on page no. 85)

3. Bhadrasana

- Sit in Vajrasana.
- Separate the knees as far as possible, while keeping the toes in contact with the floor.
- Separate the feet just enough to allow the buttocks and perineum to rest flat on the floor between the feet.
- Try to separate the knees further but do not strain.
- Place the hands on the knees, palms downward.
- When the body is comfortable, practise *nasagra drishti*, concentration on the nose tip.
- As eyes become tired close them for a short time and then resume nose tip gazing.
- Breathing should be slow and rhythmic with awareness on the breath at the nose tip.

Repetition: Repeat 2 to 3 times for 2 to 4 minutes.

Benefits: Bhadrasana alters the flow of blood and nervous impulses in the pelvic region and strengthens the pelvic muscles. It is a preventive measure as well as cure for piles. It assists women in labour.

4. Modified Katichakrasana

- Sit with legs outstretched.
- Turn the trunk slightly to the right and place the right hand behind the body, close to the left buttock, with the fingers pointing backward.
- Place the left hand on the side of the right buttock.
- Twist the head and the trunk as far to the right as is comfortable, using the arms as levers, while keeping the spine upright and straight.

- The buttocks should remain on the floor.
- Hold the final position, relaxing the back. Look over the right shoulder as far as possible.
- Re-centre the trunk, relax for a few seconds and then twist again.

Repetition: Practise up to 5 to 8 rounds and then repeat on the other side.

Breathing: Inhale before twisting. Retain the breath inside while twisting. Exhale while re-centering.

Benefits: Katichakrasana stretches the spine, and helps in loosening the vertebrae and toning the nerves. It also alleviates backache and neck pain.

5. Baalasana

- Lie down on the mat taking the left side with the fingers interlocked under the head.
- Bend the left leg sideways and bring the left knee as close to the ribs.
- The right leg should remain straight.
- Swivel the arms to the left and rest the left elbow on the floor.
- Rest the right side of the head on the crook of the right arm, or a little further down the arm for more comfort.

Baalasana

- Relax in the final pose and after some time, change side.
- The position resembles to a sleeping child.
- Breathing should be normal and relaxed in the static pose.

Repetition: Practise this asana for as long as possible on the both sides. It may also be used for sleeping and resting.

6. Anulom Vilom Pranayama

(Mentioned in The First Trimester on page no. 64)

7. Ujjai Pranayama

(Mentioned in The First Trimester on page no. 64)

8. Ashwini Mudra

- Sit in any comfortable meditation asana.
- Close the eyes and relax the body.
- Become aware of the natural breathing process for a few minutes, then take the awareness to the anus.
- Contract the sphincter muscles of the anus for a few seconds.
- Try to confine the action to the anal area.
- Repeat the practice for as long as possible.
- Contraction and relaxation should be performed smoothly and rhythmically.
- Gradually make the contraction more rapid.
- There is no limit to the duration of the practice, practise as long as it is comfortable but be careful and do not strain the muscles.

Benefits: Ashwini Mudra strengthens the anal muscles and alleviates disorders of the rectum such as constipation, piles and prolapse of the uterus or rectum.

Dietetics

Diet Therapy during Second Trimester

In the first phase of second trimester, proliferation continues and the cells already formed continue to increase in size and thus the growth of foetus takes place. This process requires amino acids and vitamin B_6, both of which are needed for synthesis of body proteins. In the second phase of this trimester cell division slows down and the growth is mainly due to increase in cell size. Therefore proteins, calcium and vitamins are the nutrients of special consideration among others.

Proper or adequate nutrition during this trimester is also necessary for proper growth of placenta. It is through the placenta that nutrients, electrolytes, water and oxygen are transferred to the foetus for its nourishment and the foetal excretory products are transferred to the maternal blood. Depending on the nutrients available in the bloodstream of the mother, placenta regulates foetal nutrition. Undernourishment of mother leads to smaller placental size and thus there are fewer cells available for the transfer of nutrients and oxygen to the foetus, leading to lower birth weight.

Specific dietary modifications during second trimester

Energy

By the second trimester of pregnancy, additional energy is required to support the growth of the foetus, development of placenta, maternal tissues and to meet the needs for increased BMR (Basal Metabolic Rate). Appropriate intake of energy is also necessary to ensure that the protein in the diet is used for body building purposes rather than for energy metabolism. ICMR has recommended an additional intake of 300kcal/day during second and third trimesters.

The best sources of energy are all cereal grains as they contain 60% to 70% of energy. Among cereals rice, wheat, bajra, ragi, jowar are exceptionally rich in energy content. Pulses also contain good amount of energy, especially soyabean, kidney beans, cow pea, green gram, Bengal gram, black gram. Nuts and oilseeds like almond, cashewnut, chilgoza, dry and fresh coconut, pistachio, gingelly seeds, mustard seeds are concentrated forms of energy. Among fruits banana, dates, black currant, dry apricot etc are rich in energy. Other than these, roots, tubers, milk and milk products especially cottage cheese, all fats and edible oils, and all sugars are rich sources of energy.

Proteins

Along with growth of foetus, development of placenta, enlargement of maternal tissues, increased maternal blood volume and formation of amniotic fluid high amounts of protein are also necessary for protein reserves required by maternal tissues to prepare for labour, delivery, the immediate postpartum period and lactation.

The daily recommended intake of protein for a pregnant woman is 65 grams per day. The rich food sources of proteins are milk and milk products, eggs, wheat germ, yeast, pulses especially soyabeans (you can also take soya milk) and legumes, green leafy vegetables, nuts and oilseeds. Milk contains very good quality protein and is rich in essential amino acid lysine. Therefore milk should necessarily be added in the diet.

Vitamins

- **Vitamin B_6 or pyridoxine:** This vitamin is important in the second trimester along with proteins. Vitamin B_6 plays an important role in the protein metabolism and in metabolism of essential fatty acids. The recommended daily intake of this vitamin during this trimester is 2.5 milligrams. The food sources of pyridoxine are vegetables, whole grain cereals, like jowar, rice, wheat whole, red gram, skimmed milk powder, whole milk powder and *khoya*. This vitamin has limited food sources; therefore, make sure to add these products in your daily diet.
- **Vitamin A:** Vitamin A requirement increases by about 25% over the usual adult intake. This requirement can be met by consuming good food sources of this vitamin which includes butter, whole cow milk, cow ghee, dark green and yellow vegetables and fruits. Animal foods such as liver, fish and egg yolk also contain this vitamin.
- **Vitamin C:** Vitamin C is greatly involved in developing the connective tissues and vascular system as well as in the absorption of iron. Citrus fruits, amla, guava, capsicum, green leafy vegetables and green chilies are good sources of vitamin C. It may be obtained in ample amounts by eating fresh fruits and drinking fresh fruit juices.
- **Vitamin D:** Vitamin D is another vitamin of great consideration as it plays an important role in the absorption and utilisation of calcium and phosphorus. As plenty of sunshine is available in our country, the requirement of vitamin D can be easily met through its bio-synthesis in the skin. Foods rich in vitamin D are butter, liver, egg-yolk and fish liver oil.

Minerals

Calcium and iron are the two much needed minerals during pregnancy. Increased calcium is required for the growth and development of the bones as well as tooth buds in the growing foetus. It is also an important constituent of the blood clotting mechanism. More calcium is needed in the second and third trimesters of pregnancy as rapid mineralisation of the skeletal tissues takes place during the period.

The daily recommended dietary intake of calcium suggested by ICMR is 1000 milligrams or 1 gram of calcium per day. This much daily intake of calcium takes care of total calcium needs of the mother and the additional needs of the foetus.

Some excellent sources of calcium are milk and milk products, like curd, *khoya*, cottage cheese. Coconut, almonds walnuts have fairly good amounts of calcium. Pulses like Bengal gram, black gram, green gram, moth beans, kidney beans, soyabean, and green leafy vegetables like amaranth leaves, colocasia leaves, fenugreek leaves, mustard leaves provide substantial amounts of calcium. Cereals too are rich sources of calcium.

Other Nutrients

Other nutrients are as essential as the nutrients mentioned above. They should be consumed in amounts as suggested by ICMR.

Special menu plan

MEAL	TIME	MENU		
		Exchange 1	*Exchange 2*	*Exchange 3*
Early Morning	6.30 am	Tea, cake rusks	Lemon tea, cookies of your choice	Tea and biscuits
Breakfast	9.00 am	Broken wheat (dalia) porridge in milk (add some dry fruits to it), cheese toast and apple	Suji porridge in milk (add some dry fruits to it), spinach besan parantha with butter, and guava	Milk, moong dal chilla with green chutney, banana
Mid-morning	11.30 am	Fresh mix fruit juice	Fresh carrot, amla, beetroot juice	Fresh pomegranate, sweet lime, pineapple juice

MEAL	TIME	MENU		
		Exchange 1	*Exchange 2*	*Exchange 3*
Lunch	1.00 pm	Chana curry, carrot and peas vegetable, spinach raita, cucumber and tomato salad and jaggery after meal	Rajma curry, lotus stem potato dry vegetable, rice, mint raita, salad of sprouts and jaggery	Rasam, sambhar, cheese masala dosa, rice, coconut chutney, sprouted moong raita, salad and jaggery after meal
After lunch	3.30 pm	Kaju barfi	Besan ka ladoo	Til-gur ka ladoo
Evening tea	5.15 pm	Banana milk shake, roasted cashew and groundnut along with pistachio and walnuts, snack of your choice	Strawberry milk shake, potato poha/ idli with tamarind chutney and roasted peanuts	Ginger and tulsi leaves tea, mix vegetable pakoras/ mix fruit chat/ sweet potato, lotus stem chaat
Dinner	8.15 pm	Spinach tomato soup, whole moong dal, bottle gourd vegetable/ stuffed tinda, chapatti/rice, fruit cream	Sweet corn soup, vegetable hakka noodles, fried rice, chilli paneer, fruit custard	Paneer peas curry, mixed vegetable dry, chapatti/rice, ice cream
Bedtime	11.00 pm	Hot almond milk	Hot almond milk	Hot almond milk

Precautions to be taken during Second Trimester

Pregnancy is the most sensitive period in the women's life cycle. It needs extra care and extra concern and lots of precautions. The first time mothers are least aware of the precautions to be taken during pregnancy. The precautions to be taken during first trimester have been mentioned in the previous section. Along with those the under mentioned precautions should also be taken during the second trimester.

1. One should be careful to avoid contamination while handling and preparing food and this is especially important for pregnant women. The pregnant lady and the cook preparing the food should wash their hands with hot soapy water before and after handling food.

Also wash the cutting boards, other work surfaces and utensils with soap and hot water after contact with raw meat, poultry or fish. These foods should always be kept separate from cooked or ready-to-eat foods. Always rinse fruits and vegetables under running tap water before eating, and remove surface dirt with a scrub brush. Remove and throw away the outermost leaves of lettuce and cabbage. Refrigerate any leftovers promptly, and never eat cooked food that has been out of the refrigerator longer than two hours. Make sure the temperature in your refrigerator is 40°F or below, and the freezer 0°F to slow down the growth of bacteria.

2. Take sufficient rest and keep stress at bay. Eat healthy, fibre-rich foods with lots of vegetables and fruits. Drink sufficient low-fat milk, yoghurt to get your calcium supply. Keep yourself hydrated by drinking lots of fluids, especially water. Go easy with fresh juices. Visit your dentist regularly. Get into regular physical activity like daily walks and swimming to keep you fit (check with your doctor first before starting anything) along with yogic workouts. Indulge in massages and warm showers to relax the muscles.
3. If you develop any of these symptoms, call your doctor or midwife immediately:
   - Blurred vision, spots, or light flashes with or without a headache
   - A hot, reddened painful area on your calf or behind your knee
   - Pain or burning when you urinate, or unusually frequent urination
   - Fever of 101°F lasting longer than 24 hours
   - Sudden severe or continuous pain or cramping in the lower abdomen
   - Bleeding or spotting from your vagina
   - Injury to your stomach
   - Sudden, severe swelling of your hands, feet or face
   - Sores or blisters on your genitals
   - Symptoms of vaginal infection — itching, burning and increase of unusual discharge
   - Continuous leaking of small amounts of fluid from the vagina or gush of water from the vagina
   - Decreased foetal movement
   - Six or more uterine contractions in one hour
   - Nausea, diarrhoea, or vomiting lasting longer than 24 hours

The Third Trimester

The third trimester covers the last three months i.e. the seventh, eigth and ninth months respectively. The trimester ends with the birth of the child. Third trimester is also called the waiting period. Mood swings and increased irritability are common during the last three months of pregnancy. Sometimes, during this period you may feel why had pregnancy stretched for such a long time? The expecting mothers probably find that though they have been feeling pretty energetic throughout their second trimester, they are beginning to slow down now; therefore, more rest periods are required. The breasts start producing ample amount of colostrum by this trimester. Some women may even find their breasts leaking. The mother feels the baby all the time as the baby begins to move regularly. Final weight gain of the pregnancy takes place. This period of pregnancy can be uncomfortable because of lot of weight gained, causing symptoms like weak bladder control and backache. Movement of the baby becomes stronger and more frequent and the baby prepares for viability outside the womb through improved brain, eye, and muscle function.

By the end of this trimester, the stomach of the mother may change shape as the baby begins to position itself for birth. The baby is prepared to become an individual and deal with the environment outside the mother's womb.

By the ninth month, lots of preparations need to be made.

Make arrangements for the hospital stay. Keep important phone numbers and papers close by. Pack the bag for the hospital, and plan how to get there at different times of the day or night. Make sure you have everything you will need when you come back home from the hospital, such as clothes and diapers.

Foetal Development in Third Trimester

Foetal Development by the End of Seventh Month

- Baby is 14 to 16 inches long and weighs between 3 to 4 pounds.
- The baby's bone marrow has now taken over the production of red blood cells.
- Due to the lack of space available to her now, baby will make fewer big movements like somersaults, and makes more small, frequent movements of the arms and legs.
- Now that almost all of the baby's organs are functioning, her growth focuses on maturing those organs and growing muscle mass and fat stores. She should more than double her weight again between now and birth.

- Taste buds develop.
- Fat layers are forming.
- Organs are maturing.
- Skin is still wrinkled and red.
- If born at this time, baby will be considered a premature baby and will require special care.

Foetal Development by the End of Eighth Month

- Baby is 16 to 18 inches long.
- Weight is about 4 to 6 pounds.
- Overall growth is rapid during this month.
- Baby is preparing for life on her own by storing iron in her liver.
- Tremendous brain growth occurs at this time.
- Most body organs are now developed with the exception of lungs.
- Movements or 'kicks' are strong enough to be visible from the outside.
- Kidneys are mature.
- Skin is less wrinkled.
- The vernix covering baby's body has become thicker.
- Fingernails now extend beyond fingertips.

Foetal Development by the End of Ninth Month

- Baby is 19 to 20 inches long.
- Weight is about 7 to 8 pounds.
- Baby is now surrounded by a peak volume of 1,000 millilitres of amniotic fluid. This is approximately equal to 4 cups.
- Baby's little knees and elbows develop dimples now.
- The lungs are matured.
- Baby is now fully developed and can survive outside the mother's body
- Skin is pink and smooth
- The cortisone is being produced by her endocrine system to help her lungs to take over the job of delivering oxygen to her blood-stream after birth.
- Baby settles down lower in the abdomen in preparation for birth and may seem less active.
- The majority of babies are now in the position, either head down (vertex) or butt down (breech), that they will maintain until birth. Any movements that they make are more likely to be rolls from side to side.

Weight Gain During Third Trimester

There are two reasons for the weight gain during third trimester of pregnancy – to nourish the developing foetus and to store up reserves for breastfeeding. The optimum pregnancy weight gain by the end of this trimester for the average woman is between 25 and 35 pounds. The total average weight gained in the third trimester is 8 to 10 pounds.

Weight gain during 30-36 weeks — 6 pounds (2.7 kg)

Weight gain during 36-38 weeks — 2 pounds (1.0 kg)

Weight gain during 38-40 weeks — Almost no weight gain

Position of the Foetus

Most babies choose a head down (vertex) position by the end of third trimester. Delivery becomes easy if the child chooses the head down position but some 3% to 4% of babies choose a head up (breech) position which makes the delivery a little complicated. There are some things that one can do at home to encourage the baby to turn to a head down position.

- The expectant mother could get on her knees and rest her chest on the floor. Hold this position for 7 to 10 minutes, several times a day.
- Hold a flashlight against the belly of the expectant mother moving it slowly toward her pubic bone in downward strokes.
- Put a small radio or a set of headphones with some gentle, interesting music against her belly, just above her pelvic bone.
- Have daddy talk to the baby with his mouth very low on mother's belly, encouraging the baby to turn down.
- Practise Setu Bandhasna and Adhomukhishwanasana.

Preparation for the Labour

The word labour pain brings goose pimples to every expecting mother. In literature and in films, childbirth is characteristically portrayed as painful and terrifying with the delivering mother shown writhing in unbearable pain. In reality, this is not true. In fact, contrary to the popular belief, while delivering in a relaxed state most mothers may not feel the labour pain as 'pain' at all. Going through the labour during pregnancy is a process of bringing your child into the world. Develop a positive feeling about labour. Prepare yourself for labour and delivery and plan for coping with it. Alleviating your anxiety about pain is one of the best ways to ensure that you will be able to deal with it when the time comes.

Pain during labour is caused primarily by uterine muscle contractions and somewhat by pressure on the cervix. This pain manifests itself as cramping in the abdomen, groin, and back, as well as a tired, achy feeling all over. Some women experience pain in their sides or thighs as well.

Other causes of pain during labour include pressure on the bladder and bowels by the baby's head and the stretching of the birth canal and vagina. Although labour is often thought of as one of the most painful events in human experience, it ranges widely from woman to woman and even from pregnancy to pregnancy.

Yoga can do wonders in this aspect by reducing the rate of labour pains thereby making the process of childbirth really easy. You can have a normal delivery without any complications and with less severity of labour pains only by performing yogic *kriyas* daily throughout the pregnancy. Along with yoga, go for regular walk and indulge yourself in daily household light activities. You can also go for swimming after consulting your doctor. Read good books and create a harmonious, feel-good environment around you.

Types of Birth

Most babies are born head downwards and facing backwards. This is the position in which the baby's head best fits the birth canal. Other positions and presentations are, however, quite common and most of them result in the successful birth of the baby provided the space in the mother's pelvis is adequate.

Other types of birth are:

Breech delivery

It is a common type of birth where the buttocks and feet emerge first.

Forceps delivery

During the second stage of labour, if the mother and baby is suffering from any problem or the mother is becoming tired, the baby is delivered with the help of surgical instruments called forceps. This type of delivery is called *forceps delivery.*

The Caesarean section

Caesarean section is another artificial means of delivering a baby. A caesarean section is commonly called a c-section. Instead of a vaginal birth, during a c-section, your baby is delivered through your abdomen. For this procedure, the doctor begins by making a small, thin incision into your abdomen. Another incision is then made into your uterus, exposing the amniotic sac that holds your baby. The baby is then gently pulled out of the uterus and welcomed into the world. Unlike instrumental delivery, this can be done in the first stage or even before labour begins. Most women prefer to give birth vaginally. Doctors also prefer this route as it minimises the amount of recovery time for mom and is the natural way for a baby to make his way into the world. The majority of caesarean sections are performed because of some difficulty arising during the labour and delivery process.

Nowadays it is a safe operation but the idea that has developed in some circles that the caesarean section is an easy way to have a baby is false. It is followed by discomforts and risks that follow with any surgery, for example, organs close to uterus like the kidney and bladder may be infected, there is an increased blood loss which is about twice as much blood as with a vaginal birth. Baby can also experience some problems associated with a caesarean delivery. Babies born through caesarean section tend to have a greater chance of having respiratory problems. Most women who have had babies with both methods prefer the normal way.

Common Complications during Third Trimester

1. Backache

Backache is very common in pregnancy. Almost 70% of all pregnant women deal with some sort of back pain. Backaches often occur as the increasing weight pulls the spine forward and shifts expecting mother's centre of gravity. During pregnancy, the pelvic joints relax in order to increase the size and flexibility of the pelvis in preparation for birth. This may cause pressure on the sciatic nerve and may lead to pain in the pelvic area, down the thigh and into the leg. There are ligaments that hold the uterus in place – one is on both sides of the uterus and a third going across the pelvic floor. As the uterus grows, these ligaments stretch like a rubberband. Any sudden movement or position change can cause them to spasm.

The ligaments become softer and stretch to prepare for labour. As the baby grows, the hollow in the back of lady may increase and this may cause backache. Also, due to the increased weight, the muscles in your back may have to work harder to support your balance, resulting in increased lower back pain. Fortunately, there are lots of simple yogic activities which can help in backache.

Precautions to be taken

1. First, consider the possibility of backache as a symptom of pre-term labour.
2. Practise good posture and stand straight and tall with your backbone straight.
3. Always be careful while lifting objects. Bend your knees instead of bending over at the waist. Lift with your legs instead of your back.
4. Wear supportive shoes with low heels. Avoid standing for long periods of time.
5. Put one foot on a step stool to relieve back stress while standing.
6. Consider wearing a maternity support belt to help relieve some of the pressure.
7. Maternity pants with a low, supportive waistband may also be helpful.
8. Apply heat using warm bath soaks, warm wet towels, a hot water bottle or heating pad.
9. Get a back massage and take proper rest.

Yoga therapy for backache during pregnancy

1. Chakki Chalanasana (churning the mill posture)

- Sit with legs outstretched in front of your body about one foot apart.
- Interlock the fingers of both hands and hold the arms out straight in front of the chest.
- Keep the arms straight and horizontal throughout the practice. Do not bend the elbows.
- Bend forward as far as possible comfortably without any jerk.
- Imagine the action of churning a mill with a stone grinder.
- Swivel to the right so that the hands pass above the right toes and as far to the right as possible.
- Lean back as far as possible on the backward swing.
- Try to move the body from the waist. On the forward swing, bring the arms and hands to the left side, over the left toes and then back to the centre position.
- One rotation is one round.
- Practise 5 to 10 rounds clockwise then the same number of rounds anti-clockwise.

Chakki Chalanasana

Breathing: Inhale while leaning back and exhale while moving forward.

Benefits: This asana is excellent for toning the nerves and organs of the pelvis and abdomen. This is also a good exercise for relieving back pain.

2. Modified Katichakrasana

(Mentioned in The Second Trimester on page no. 92)

3. Setu Bandhasana (the bridge posture)

- Lie flat on the knees, placing the soles of the feet flat on the floor with the heels touching the buttocks.
- The feet and knees may be hip width apart.
- Grasp the ankles with the hands.
- This is the starting position.
- Raise the buttocks and arch the back upward.
- Try to raise the chest and navel as high as possible, pushing the chest up towards the chin and head without moving the position of the feet or shoulders.
- Keep the feet flat on the floor.

- In the final position, the body is supported by the head, neck, shoulders, arms and feet.
- Hold the pose for as long as is comfortable and then lower the body to the starting position.
- Release the ankles and relax with legs outstretched.
- Practise 5 to 10 rounds.

Breathing: Inhale deeply in the starting position. Retain the breath inside while raising and holding the final position. Alternatively, breathe slowly and deeply in the final position. Exhale while lowering to the starting position.

Benefits: This asana is a boon for people suffering from backache. It is also utilised to realign the spine, eliminating rounded shoulders and it has successfully been used to turn the baby when it is a breech presentation.

4. Prashtha Sparshasana

- Lie flat on the back with knees bent, placing the soles of the feet flat on the floor with the heels touching the buttocks.
- Keep the feet and knees hip width apart.
- Try to grasp the ankles with the hands. If not comfortable put the hands facing down near the buttocks.
- Now touch the curved portion of your back to the ground which usually remains untouched because of the curve in the spinal cord.
- This is the final position. Stay in the position as long as you are comfortable.
- Breathing should be normal.

Benefits: It relieves back pain and relaxes the spine.

2. Oedema (Swelling in legs, feet and hands)

During pregnancy, it is normal to experience swelling in the feet, legs and hands that makes the skin feel tight. The amount of blood in body increases about 40%. In addition, the body naturally holds water. The heart needs to work harder to circulate this extra fluid. For about one out of three women, swelling of the hands and feet occurs during the last three months of pregnancy and is often greater during hot weather. Some swelling or puffiness is not unusual or serious, but it can be uncomfortable.

> *"I used to experience lot of pain and swelling in the lower part of my legs and feet due to the weight gain during 6 months of my pregnancy. Nishtha then suggested a few yogic exercises for my legs and feet and also charted out a special diet plan. I stuck to it for a week or so and found excellent results. Not only the pain and swelling subsided considerably, but I could now walk and move more comfortably than before. Never knew simple things like yoga and diet could do wonders."*
>
> — Meeta H Bhogayata, Nagpur

Yoga therapy for oedema during pregnancy

1. For hands

a) Mushtika Bandh (hand clenching)

- Sit in Vajrasana or in any other cross-legged pose.
- Hold both the arms straight in front of the body at shoulder level.
- Open the hands and palms down, and stretch the fingers as wide apart as possible.
- Close the fingers to make a tight fist with the thumbs inside.
- The fingers should be slowly wrapped around the thumb.
- Again open the hand and stretch the fingers.
- Repeat 10 times.

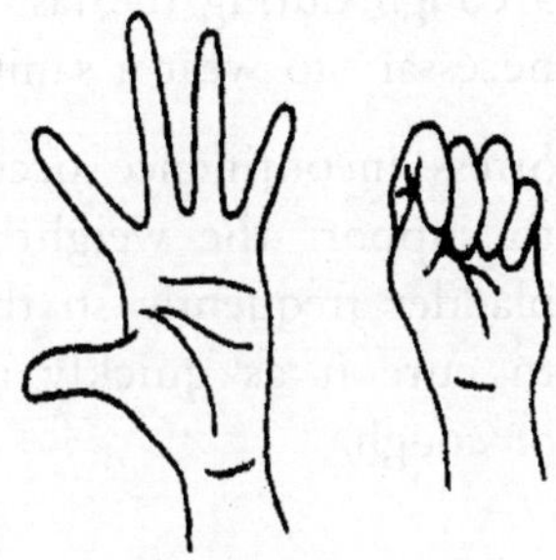

Mushtika Bandh

Breathing: Inhale on opening the hands. Exhale on closing the hands.

b) Manibandh Chakra (wrist joint rotation)

- Remain in the same sitting pose and keep the back straight.
- Extend both arms in front of the body make the fist clenched with thumb inside.
- Keep the arms straight and at shoulder level.
- Rotate the fist together first clockwise and then anti-clockwise.
- Practise 10 times each direction.

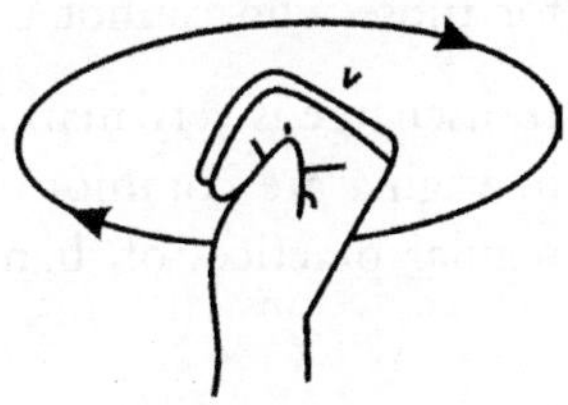

Manibandh Chakra

2. For feet and legs

(Mentioned in The Second Trimester)

Diet therapy for oedema during pregnancy

- Eat foods high in protein, such as beans, cheese, fish, meat, poultry and tofu.
- Try to avoid standing for long periods of time.
- Drink the fresh juice of a lemon in a cup of warm water to help decrease the extra fluid your body retains.

Other suggestions

- Rest two or three times a day with your legs elevated higher than your heart. Lie down with pillows under your calves and feet.
- Lying down on your left side is better for circulation.
- Avoid wearing tight clothes like pants, stockings etc. Varicose veins may be associated with swelling.
- Exercise regularly by walking or swimming.
- Try submerging in water up to your shoulders. The water should be no warmer than body temperature.
- Check your fluid intake.

3. Stress Incontinence

This is the involuntary passing of urine during coughing and straining. A woman who develops a cough during the last week of pregnancy is particularly liable to suffer from it and may find it necessary to wear a sanitary pad. Even laughing may cause this problem.

Stress incontinence occurs because the muscles supporting the bladder are not strong enough to support the weight of the uterus, which is pushed by any sort of straining. Empty the bladder frequently so that you are able to control it. If you develop a cough, get your doctor to cure it as quickly as possible. Remember to tighten up your muscles before you laugh or cough.

4. Vaginal Discharge

Most pregnant women have a slight discharge during pregnancy. In some cases one has to change panties several times a day. Panties of a more absorbent material such as cotton are more satisfactory for those who cannot change during the day.

If discharge is very marked or it irritates or is offensive in odour, consult your doctor. Slight infections in vagina are common during pregnancy because of the increased acidity of the vagina. With the regular practices of '**bandhas**' you will not face this problem during your pregnancy.

5. Insomnia

Insomnia is the complete loss of sleep, difficulty in falling asleep, difficulty in staying asleep, early awakening or a combination of any of these complaints.

It is caused due to mental tension brought about by anxiety, worries, overwork and over-excitement in expecting mothers. Other causes are constipation, overeating at night or going to bed on empty stomach, excessive intake of starches, tea or coffee.

Yoga therapy for insomnia

1. Makarasana

- Lie on stomach.
- Stretch both arms above the head with the palms facing downward. The forehead should be resting on the floor.
- Relax the whole body in the same way as described in Shavasana.
- If there is difficulty in breathing or a sense of suffocation is experienced, a pillow may be placed under the chest.

Breathing: Natural and rhythmic

Duration: 10 to 15 minutes

2. Baalasana
   (Mentioned in The Second Trimester on page no. 92)

3. Shavasana
   (Mentioned in Infertility and Inability to Conceive on page no. 43)

5. Rhythmic Breathing
   - Sit in any comfortable meditation posture.
   - Observe the natural and spontaneous breathing process.
   - Develop total awareness of the rhythmic flow of the breath.
   - Feel the breath flowing in and out at the back of the mouth above the throat.
   - Bring the awareness down to the region of the throat and feel the breath flowing in the throat.
   - Bring the awareness down to the region of chest and feel the breath flowing in the trachea and the bronchial tubes.
   - Next feel the breath flowing in the lungs.
   - Be aware of lungs expanding and relaxing.
   - Shift the attention to the ribcage and observe the expansion and relaxation of this area.
   - Bring the awareness down to the abdomen. Feel the abdomen move upward on inhalation and downward on exhalation.
   - Finally become aware of whole breathing process from the nostrils to abdomen and continue observing it for some time.
   - Bring the awareness back to observing the physical body as one unit and open the eyes.
   - Practise for 5 to 10 minutes.

Diet therapy for insomnia

Diet plays a key role in the treatment of insomnia. Researches show that the deficiency of some nutrients i.e. vitamin C, vitamin D, vitamins B complex, magnesium, potassium, calcium, zinc and manganese leads to insomnia. To overcome insomnia, exclude white flour products, tea, coffee, chocolates, soft drinks and fried foods from your diet. Foods containing additives, preservatives, flavouring and colouring, excessive salt should also be avoided. Add a plenty of fresh fruits mainly juicy fruits and fresh fruit juices and celery soup to your daily diet. While going to bed, take a glass of warm milk sweetened with honey. Take your dinner before 8 pm as meals taken late in the night lead to insomnia.

Helpful suggestions

- Create a comfortable environment. Make your bedroom quiet, cool and dark.
- Massage your head with curd before bath.
- Do not take naps during the day.
- Inhale deep fresh air while walking in the garden in the evening.

Yoga

Regular Yogic Workouts during Third Trimester

1. Greeva Sanchalana (neck movements)

Stage 1

- Stand straight with feet together.
- Close the eyes.
- Slowly move the head forward and try to touch the chin to the chest.
- Move the head as far back as comfortable. Do not strain.
- Try to feel the stretch of the muscles in the front and back of the neck, and the loosening of the vertebrae in the neck.
- Practise 10 times.

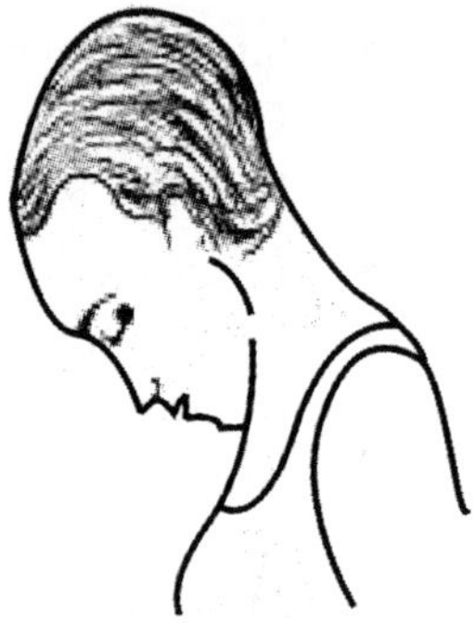

Breathing: Inhale in the backward movement and exhale in the forward movement.

Stage 2

- Remain in the same position, keeping the eyes closed.
- Face directly forward. Relax the shoulders.
- Slowly move the head to the right and try to touch the right ear to the right shoulder without turning the head or raising the shoulders.
- Move the head to the left side and try to touch the left ear to the left shoulder.
- This is one round.
- Do not strain; touching the shoulder is not necessary.
- Practise 10 rounds.

Breathing: Inhale on the upward movement. Exhale on the downward movement.

Stage 3

- Remain in the same position.
- Keep the head upright and the eyes closed.
- Slowly rotate the head downward, to the right, backward and then to the left side in a relaxed smooth rhythmic circular movement.
- Feel the shifting stretch around the neck and the loosening of the joints and muscles of the neck.
- Practise 10 times clockwise and then 10 times anti-clockwise.

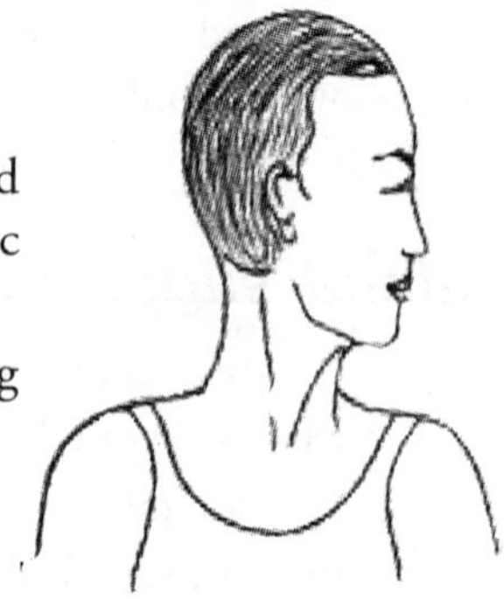

- Do not strain. If the dizziness occurs, open the eyes. After the practice, keep the neck straight and the eyes closed. Be aware of the sensations in the head and neck.

Breathing: Inhale as the head moves up and exhale as the head moves down.

Benefits: All the nerves connecting the different organs and limbs of the body pass through the neck. Therefore the muscles of the neck and shoulders accumulate tension, especially in pregnancy because of gained weight. These asanas release tension, heaviness and stiffness in the head, neck and shoulder region.

2. Manibandh Chakra

(Mentioned in Yoga therapy for oedema during pregnancy on page no. 105)

3. Skandh Chakra

- Stand straight on your mat with your feet together.
- Place the fingers of the right hand on the right shoulder.
- And the fingers of the left hand on the left shoulder.
- Fully rotate both elbows at the same time in a large circle.
- Try to touch the elbows in front of chest on the forward movement and touch the sides of the trunk while coming down.
- Practise only 10 times clockwise and then 10 times anti-clockwise.

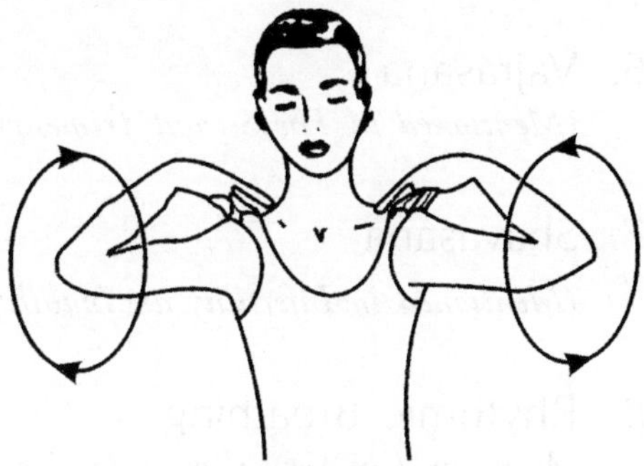

Skandh Chakra

Benefits: It relieves the strain and maintain the shape of breasts.

4. Padmasana

(Mentioned in The First Trimester on page no. 70)

5. Titli Asana (butterfly posture)

- Sit with the legs outstretched.
- Place the palms of the hands on the floor to the sides and just behind the buttocks.
- Bend the knees and bring the soles of the feet together, keeping the heels as close to the body as possible.
- Fully relax the inner thigh muscles.

Titli Asana

Stage 1
- Clasp the feet with both hands.
- Gently bounce the knees up and down, using the elbows as levers to press the legs down.
- Try to touch the knees to the ground on the downward stroke.
- Do not use any force.
- Practise 30 to 50 ups and downs.

Stage 2
- Keep the soles of the feet together.
- Place the hands on the knees.
- Using the palms, gently push the knees down towards the floor, allowing them to spring up again.
- Do not force this movement.
- Repeat 20 to 30 times.
- Straighten the legs and relax.

Breathing: Normal breathing

Benefits: It prepares the body for normal delivery.

6. Vajrasana

(Mentioned in The Second Trimester on page no. 87)

7. Shavasana

(Mentioned in Infertility an Inability to Conceive on page no. 43)

8. Rhythmic Breathing

(Mentioned in Yoga therapy for insomnia on page no. 107)

9. Sheetali Pranayama

- Sit in any comfortable meditation posture with hands on knees in Gyan Mudra.
- Close the eyes and relax the body.
- Extend the tongue outside the mouth as far as possible without strain.
- Roll the sides of the tongue up so that it forms a tube. Inhale and draw the breath in through this tube.
- At the end of inhalation, draw the tongue in, close the mouth and exhale through the nose.
- The breath should produce a noise similar to rushing wind.

Sheetali Pranayama

- A feeling of ice coldness will be experienced on the tongue and the roof of the mouth.
- This is one round.
- Practise 9 rounds. Gradually increase the number of rounds from 9 to 15 and the duration of each inhalation/exhalation.

Precautions: This technique should not be practised in a dirty polluted atmosphere or during cold weather.

Benefits: This practice cools the body and mind. It affects the brain centres associated with biological derives and temperature regulation. It cools and reduces mental and emotional excitation (which is common in last trimester of pregnancy), and encourages the free flow of *'prana'* throughout the body. It induces muscular relaxation, mental tranquillity and may be used as a tranquilliser before sleep. If you are suffering from insomnia or lack of sleep, this technique is of great relief. It also helps reduce blood pressure and acid stomach.

10. Sahajoli Mudra

- Sit in any comfortable cross-legged meditation posture with head and spine straight.
- Place hands on the knees in Gyan Mudra.
- Close the eyes and relax the body.
- Take the awareness to urethra.
- Inhale and hold the breath in and try to draw the urethra upward. This muscle action is similar to holding back an intense urge to urinate.
- The labia in women should move slightly due to this contraction.
- Try to focus and confine the force of the contraction at the urethra. Bending a little forward during the contraction helps to isolate this point.
- Hold the contraction for as long as comfortable.
- Exhale while releasing the contraction and relax.
- Practise twice more.

Duration: Hold the contraction for as long as is comfortable, starting with a few seconds and gradually increasing. Begin with three contractions and slowly increase up to 10 to 15 rounds.

Benefits: This mudra regulates and tones the entire uro-genital system, correcting incontinence and recurrent urinary tract infections. Sahajoli corrects uterine prolapse.

11. Mool bandha

(Mentioned in Pre-Pregnancy on page no. 32)

12. Meditation

(Mentioned in Pre-Pregnancy on page no. 33)

Dietetics

Specific Dietary Requirements during Third Trimester

The third trimester is mainly the period of growth. Requirements of the nutrients at this time are high, both quantitatively and qualitatively. Nutritional deficiencies during this period usually result in premature deliveries and low-birth-weight babies. The nutritional requirements during this trimester are almost same as in second trimester because this trimester is an extension of the second trimester only. But along with them the intake of a few other important nutrients are necessary because at this time mother has to prepare herself for the delivery also. Therefore along with proteins, energy, iron, calcium, vitamin B and vitamin C, vitamin K also comes up as a very important nutrient for this trimester.

Specific dietary modifications during third trimester

(Same as mentioned under 'Specific dietary modifications during second trimester in section 5)

Vitamin K

Vitamin K is required for the synthesis of a protein called prothrombin which is essential for the normal coagulation of blood in the body. The speed with which the blood clots after surgery depends on the amount of vitamin K in the body. Therefore, the proper intake of this vitamin during this trimester is necessary to prevent neonatal haemorrhages and to cope up with the loss of blood during delivery. It has, therefore, become a routine practice to give natural form of this vitamin by injection to the mother prior to delivery or to the neonate soon after birth. The best sources of this vitamin are all green leafy vegetables, like cabbage, lettuce, spinach and carrot greens. Animal foods such as egg yolk, milk and organ meats like liver also contain a good amount of this vitamin.

Special menu plan

MEAL	TIME	MENU		
		Exchange 1	*Exchange 2*	*Exchange 3*
Early Morning	6.30 am	Lemon tea, cookies of your choice	Tea, cake rusks	Tea and biscuits
Breakfast	9.00 am	Cashewnut milk shake, pea potato stuffed toast (wheat bread) and apple	Vegetable besan chilla with coriander mint chutney, milk and guava	Broken wheat (dalia) porridge in milk, paneer stuffed parantha

MEAL	TIME	MENU		
		Exchange 1	*Exchange 2*	*Exchange 3*
Mid-morning	11.30 am	Fresh mix fruit juice	Fresh carrot, amla beetroot juice	Fresh pomegranate, sweet lime, pineapple juice
Lunch	1.00 pm	Whole urad dal, mix vegetable, spinach raita, chapatti, cucumber and tomato salad, and jaggery after meal	Vegetable sambhar, methi mutter malai vegetable, stuffed capsicum (stuffed with potato, cheese and peas mixture), chapatti, rice, and jaggery after meal, cucumber raita, sprouts salad	Channa curry, cauliflower potato vegetable, chapatti, rice, bottle gourd raita, green salad, and jaggery after meal
After lunch	3.30 pm	Milk Cake	Besan ka ladoo	Til gur ka ladoo
Evening tea	5.15 pm	Banana milkshake, roasted cashew and groundnut along with pistachio and walnuts, vegetable cutlets	Strawberry milkshake, vegetable upma/ idli with tamarind chutney and roasted peanuts	Cashew milkshake, mix vegetable pakoras/ mix fruit chat/ sweet potato, lotus stem chaat
Dinner	8.15 pm	Mix vegetable pulao, pineapple raita, potato stuffed parantha, moong dal halwa	Spinach tomato soup, bottle gourd kofta curry, methi carrot potato vegetable, chapatti, rice, fruit cream	Sweet corn soup, vegetable hakka noodles, fried rice, chilli paneer, fruit custard
Bedtime	11.00 pm	Hot almond milk	Hot almond milk	Hot almond milk

Precautions to be taken during Third Trimester

(Same as explained in first and second trimester)

Yogic Techniques for Normal Delivery

There are some yogic techniques which can ensure a normal delivery if practised regularly in the ninth month till the date of delivery.

1. Chakki Chalanasana

(Mentioned in Yoga Therapy for Backache on page no. 103)

2. Kak Gati

- Sit in squatting position with the feet apart and the buttocks above the heels.
- Place the palms of the hands on the knees.
- Take small steps in the squatting position.
- Try to keep the knees flexed so that the buttocks are not moved away from the heels walk either on the toes or the soles of feet, which ever is comfortable.
- As you take a step forward bring the opposite knee to the floor.
- Take as many steps as possible, up to 20, and then relax in Shavasana.

Breathing: Normal breathing

Kak Gati

3. Adhomukhi Shwanasana

(5th step of Surya Namaskar)

- Stand with spine erect, feet together and hands beside the body. Relax the body.
- Distribute the weight of the body evenly on both feet.
- Slowly bend forward, first bending the head, taking the chin towards the chest, then bending the upper trunk, relaxing the shoulders forward and letting the arms go limp.
- Bend the mid trunk and finally the lower trunk.
- While bending forward imagine that the body has no bones or muscles. Do not strain or force the body.

Adhomukhi Shwanasana

- Bring the fingertips as near to the floor as possible.
- Relax the back of the neck and bend it loosely towards the knees.
- Do not try to touch the forehead to the knees.
- Take the left foot back beside the right foot simultaneously, raise the buttocks and lower the head between the arms, so that the back and the legs form two sides of a triangle.
- Legs and arms should be straight in the final position.
- Try to keep the heels on the floor and bring the head towards the knees.
- Do not strain yourself. Hold the position as long as you are comfortable.
- Repeat 3 times.

Yoga and the Childbirth Process

The months have flown by and now it is almost time for the baby to arrive! You have probably created a birth plan by now and are eagerly anticipating meeting your new little one. But now is also an emotional time for you and you may be experiencing worries and fears about your labour and delivery. Many pregnant women especially first time pregnant come to me and ask what they should expect and do at the moment of birth. They are often apprehensive about this event because they think that giving birth is extremely risky and dangerous, and whatever happens, childbirth causes the mother great physical pain.

The practice of yoga helps the future mother to overcome her fear and prepare her effectively for the event. Yoga remedies this by constituting a discipline, which teaches mother-to-be how to remain calm and self-controlled, and how to relax and breathe correctly during the different stages of childbirth.

The mother should avoid resistance, fear and irritation, for allowing everything to happen calmly and serenely. A woman, who is tensed, will feel pain because she is resisting and thereby hindering the child from emerging. Such a state of mind leads to genital tension and causes suffering by blocking the smooth, painless birth of the infant. The practice of yoga develops the ability to relax once the contractions begin, stills the future mother's fear, and helps her learn the required patience and calm so that she can co-operate more effectively at the moment of birth. The more confidence and self-control she possesses, the less pain she will feel.

Childbirth normally takes place in three stages:

1. Dilation
2. Expulsion
3. Delivery

1. Dilation or Opening-Up

This is the stage where the mouth of the uterus opens fully so that it can accommodate the head of the baby and allow the baby to pass down the genital canal at the moment of birth. The mouth of the uterus dilates as a result of the contractions of the uterine muscles.

Yogic activity during this period

At the beginning of the opening-up period, when the contractions are infrequent and not very strong, the mother should relax, while at the same time practising deep abdominal breathing also called yogic breathing. Between contractions, you should try to continue breathing deeply and regularly, for on a physical level, this will ensure the optimal oxygen supply required for yourself and the baby. This technique of deep rhythmic breathing ensures a harmonious functioning of the whole system including the brain, and helps, on a psychological level, to calm the emotions and create a feeling of well-being. When the contractions continue for a longer period and become more frequent, you should avoid abdominal breathing, and simply perform middle chest breathing.

2. Expulsion

The transition between the full opening of the mouth of the uterus and the birth of the baby is known as expulsion. It lasts some 10 to 20 minutes, but can be longer or shorter.

Yogic activity during this period

Throughout the period of expulsion, the mother should push during contractions and relax between them, in order to muster your energy for when you next push. At this point, having exhaled, you should inhale deeply, and with full lungs and a closed mouth and glottis, contract the abdominal muscles and push. Exhalation through the mouth should sound like a sigh of relief. An effective way of continuing to push is to exhale slowly through the nose, making sure the glottis is partly closed. You should push against your breath when contracting the abdominal muscles and lowering the diaphragm. This way of adjusting the glottis is taught in this book while practising Ujjai Pranayama. It enables you to regulate the amount of air you exhale and to push longer without becoming out of breath or using up energy in vain. As you let out the breath through the nose, a low continuous sound is emitted. When the head is expelled, you should inhale and exhale, deeply and regularly performing middle and upper-chest respiration (without abdominal breathing). Following the instructions of the doctor or midwife, the mother should then resume pushing slightly, so that the rest of the child's body slips out, and the baby is born. This is the third stage of childbirth called ***Delivery***.

> *"I was very scared as I had heard so much about the pain a mother-to-be has to undergo during the process of delivering the baby. Then I took to yoga completely during my last days of pregnancy. The breathing techniques that I learnt from Nishtha and practised during that time helped me immensely during labour and unbelievably I felt almost no pain during the delivery! And before I could actually realise the baby was there."*
>
> — Sonia Jain, Kolkata

Post-Pregnancy

The Lying-in Period

It was not so long ago when a woman used to stay in bed for a month or forty days after giving birth to a baby. It was believed that not taking enough rest during the first few weeks may lead to permanent disabilities.

It has been now established that this is not true. Most women recover from the effects of labour within a few hours after having a sound sleep though some women may take a bit longer after an exhaustive labour.

A woman needs to adjust after the delivery of the baby both physically and mentally. A woman stays in a highly emotional state just after the delivery and requires protection from the normal stresses and strains of life. However, bearing all this in mind, it is best to regard the lying-in period as a necessity.

Nowadays women are often advised to get up on the first or second day after taking rest. A moderate amount of activity almost from the start helps the muscles and the womb to become normal and prevents the likelihood of thrombosis in the veins. A moderate amount of activity is good for health and moderate amount of rest is good for mental and emotional well-being and also for the milk supply, therefore there is a need to strike balance between the two.

Getting Adjusted to New Changes

With the arrival of the baby, there is an additional responsibility. After all these weeks of agonising wait, preparation and planning, you have your baby in your arms. The initial period after birth brings a lot of changes in your life and you have to prepare yourself to adjust to changes smartly.

One important thing to be kept in mind during this period is to try to make time for your husband. Often it is a new father who faces mental turbulence during the days immediately following the birth of the baby. He needs your support as much as you need his. Talk to each other about your feelings and let him share the responsibility in looking after the baby. After the initial fumbling and hiccups, he will learn to handle the baby perfectly.

The early weeks with your newborn are a time to learn to adjust to each other as a family. You will be giving a lot of energy to your baby in the beginning. If this does not come naturally to you, think of it as an important investment that will pay off in the future. Focus on the good feelings you get when you and your baby are close. Be easy on yourself. Parenting a newborn is hard work, but it is rewarding, as was labour and childbirth.

Your priority is to get to know your baby by learning to read and respond appropriately to her cues. Leave everything else to someone else. When friends and family offer to help, let them do your chores, or just let your chores wait.

Many new parents, particularly mothers, experience mild depression and some go through severe depression post-pregnancy. This seems to be a reaction to all the excitement involved in childbirth and is probably related to the hormonal changes taking place in the body as it adjusts to its post-pregnancy stage. Depression can also come in those mothers who are used to a more active lifestyle. They feel tied up by their young babies in the home.

Yoga and a balanced diet is the answer to most such problems post-pregnancy.

Common Problems Post-pregnancy

1. Piles

It is one of the common problems of pregnancy. This occurs mostly due to the fact that in Indian society a new mother is fed with lot of eatables which contain dry fruits and condiments, an overdose of which may lead to the problem, such as piles. Not to worry though, regular practice of yoga helps cure this problem. Yoga therapy for piles should be started only after the completion of 40 days rest period.

Yoga therapy for piles

1. Gupta Padmasana
   (Mentioned in Infertility and Inability to Conceive on page no. 53)

2. Sarvangasana
   (Mentioned in Pre-Pregnancy on page no. 26)

3. Halasana
   (Mentioned in Pre-Pregnancy on page no. 27)

4. Ashwini Mudra
   (Mentioned in The Second Trimester on page no. 93)

Diet therapy for piles

Consume light, easily digestible foods, fresh fruits and vegetables. Drink plenty of water, fruit and vegetable juices, herbal teas. Avoid non-vegetarian food and heavy foods like cheese, fried or oily food, rich sauces and desserts. Spices are a complete 'NO' to a person who is suffering from piles.

2. Excessive Bleeding

Lochia is the name given to postpartum bleeding. Every woman who delivers a child, either vaginally or through caesarean section will experience this type of bleeding. It is the way in which your body expels excess mucus, placental tissue and blood after giving birth.

Lochia is very similar to the bleeding you experience during your menstrual period but it is much heavier. It typically begins in the hours immediately following birth and usually continues for two or three weeks. However, in some women lochia can last for up to six weeks. It is noticed that in some women the bleeding is unusually heavy, which is not normal and can lead to postpartum haemorrhaging. In such cases, consult your doctor immediately. Yoga therapy prescribed here will be of immense help in making the flow normal and stopping it early.

Helpful suggestions

- Rest as much as you can, and avoid excess standing and walking (this will exacerbate the blood flow).
- Use heavy duty maxi pads to soak up the blood.
- Do not use tampons for at least six weeks after pregnancy. Tampons can introduce bacteria into the vagina and uterus, causing infection.

Yoga therapy for excessive bleeding

Yoga therapy for excessive bleeding should be started only after 10 days of delivery (if it is a normal one). For mothers with caesarean delivery only *'Mool Bandha'* is suggested.

1. Sarvangasana

   (Mentioned in Pre-Pregnancy on page no. 27)

2. Mool Bandha

   (Mentioned in Pre-Pregnancy on page no. 32)

Diet therapy for excessive bleeding

Excessive postpartum bleeding can lead to severe cases of anaemia. To avoid the loss and for fast recovery, add all types of fruits and fruit juices, lot of milk and milk products, green leafy vegetables and eggs to your diet. For more details refer to the diet therapy for anaemia under section 4.

3. Stretch Marks

When a person gains weight suddenly, the skin expands to accommodate the increase in body weight. Skin is elastic and can be stretched to a certain limit. Once the limit is crossed, the innermost layer of the skin tears as it can stretch no more. As the underlying layer tears and the ones above are intact, the skin appears to be streaked. As soon as the skin tears, pink or purple lines appear as the capillaries burst. After some time these lines look slivery white. These are called stretch marks, which are in fact scars that are a result of skin tearing.

Most of the women develop stretch marks during pregnancy. As you put on weight, the abdomen (stomach) is gradually stretched further and further, usually causing stretch marks to appear in the sixth or seventh month. Stretch marks can also appear on the thighs, abdomen, hips, breasts and upper arms as they get bigger and heavier.

Yoga therapy for stretch marks

Yoga therapy for stretch marks should only be started after the completion of 2 months of delivery in case of normal delivery and after 3 months in case of caesarean delivery.

1. Sarvang Pushti
   (Mentioned in Infertility and Inability to Conceive on page no. 36)

2. Surya Namaskar
   (Mentioned in Pre-Pregnancy on page no. 20)

3. Dhanurasana
   (Mentioned in Infertility and Inability to Conceive on page no. 50)

4. Chakrasana
   (Mentioned in Infertility and Inability to Conceive on page no. 50)

5. Uttanpadasana
   (Mentioned in Pre-Pregnancy on page no. 25)

Diet therapy for stretch marks

Eat foods rich in zinc like nuts and fish, foods with a high content of vitamin A, C, and D like citrus fruits, dairy products, carrots and protein-rich foods like eggs can improve the quality of your skin and can cure stretch marks. Drink plenty of water, at least 8-10 glasses per day. Adequate water intake will make your skin soft and supple thus preventing it from tearing. Reduce intake of tea, coffee and carbonated drinks. Eat nutritious food and maintain a healthy diet to keep your skin young and healthy and prevent stretch marks.

4. Lack of Sleep

After delivery due to changed surroundings and life style many mothers come under depression and face stress. They are not able to have proper sleep and hardly get time to sleep in quest of meeting the demands of the new born. All these factors lead to frustration. In yoga therapy, there are some *kriyas* which can complete the sleep cycle of 7 hours in 30 minutes.

Yoga therapy for lack of sleep

(Same as suggested for insomnia in section 6 – the third trimester. Practise these asanas and experience the miracle)

5. Pigmentation or Chloasma

Pigmentation or patches of darker skin on the skin post-pregnancy is very common and absolutely normal. According to the American Academy of Dermatology, up to 70% of pregnant women develop blotchy areas of darkened skin, commonly called the mask of pregnancy. These changes are caused by hormonal changes during pregnancy, which stimulate a temporary increase in the body's production of melanin, the natural substance that gives colour to hair, skin, and eyes. The areas of increased pigmentation will probably fade within a few months after delivery and the skin should return to its normal shade, although in some women the changes never completely disappear.

Women with darker complexions are more prone to this condition than women with lighter skin. The pigmentation can show up around your upper lip, nose, cheekbones, and forehead, cheeks or along the jaw line. You may develop dark patches on your forearms and other parts of your body that are exposed to the sun.

Helpful suggestions

- Be regular with your yoga schedule (prescribed in this book) throughout the pregnancy and see the miracle! You will not face this problem.
- Protect yourself from the sun. This is crucial because exposure to the sun's ultraviolet (UV) rays intensifies pigment changes.
- Use a broad-spectrum sunblock with SPF 30 or higher every day, whether it is sunny or not, and reapply often during the course of the day if you are outside.
- Use gentle cleansers and facial creams.
- Apply a concealing make-up.
- Do not use skin-bleaching products until the pigmentation goes away.

Yoga

Regular Yogic Workouts Post-pregnancy

Mothers with normal delivery can start these regular yogic workouts within a week, whereas mothers with caesarean section delivery should wait for at least two months or till they recover from the after effects of the surgery. It is always advisable to consult your doctor before starting any physical activity.

Week 1

1. Sugam Sarpasana

- Lie flat on stomach with the forehead resting on the floor, the legs straight, feet together, and the soles of feet facing the sky.
- Bend the arms and place the forearms on the floor with the palms downward on each side of the head.
- The fingertips point forward but are inline with the crown of the head.
- The forearms and elbows are close to the body.
- Relax the whole body.
- Raise the head, shoulders and chest by bringing the upper arms to the vertical position.
- The elbows, forearms and hands will remain on the floor.
- Relax in the position for a comfortable length of time and then slowly lower the body.
- This is one round.

Duration: Try to hold the position for 3 to 4 minutes as a static pose.

Breathing: Inhale while raising the head, shoulders and chest. Exhale while lowering to the floor. Breathe normally in the final position.

Benefits: This asana tones ovaries and uterus, and helps alleviate menstrual and other gynecological disorders. It stimulates the appetite, alleviates constipation and is beneficial for all abdominal organs. The adrenal glands are gently massaged and stimulated. The secretion of cortisone is maintained and the thyroid gland is regulated. This asana can relocate slipped disc, remove backache and keep the spine supple and healthy.

2. Bilav Asana (cat posture)

- Sit in Vajrasana.
- Raise the buttocks and stand on the knees.
- Lean forward and place the hands flat on the floor beneath the shoulders with the fingers facing forward.

Bilav Asana

- The hands should be in line with the knees, the arms and thighs should be perpendicular on the floor.
- The knees may be together or slightly separated.
- This is the starting position.
- Inhale while raising the head and depressing the spine so that the back becomes concave.
- Expand the abdomen fully and fill the lungs with the maximum amount of air.
- Hold the breath for three seconds.
- Exhale while lowering the head and stretching the spine upward.
- At the end of exhalation contract the abdomen and pull in the buttocks.
- The head will now be between the arms, facing the thighs.
- Hold the breath for three seconds, accentuating the arch of the spine and the spinal contraction.
- This is one round.

Breathing: Try to perform the movement breathing as slowly as possible. Aim at taking at least 5 seconds for both inhalation and exhalation.

Repetition: Perform 5 to 10 rounds.

Benefits: This asana gently tones the female reproductive system. Women suffering from menstrual disorders and leucorrhea shall obtain relief by doing bilav asana. It may also be practised during menstruation for relief from cramps.

3. Baalasana

(Mentioned in The Second Trimester on page no. 92)

Week 2

1. Greeva Sanchalana

(Mentioned in The Third Trimester on page no. 108)

2. Manibandh Chakra

(Mentioned in The Third Trimester on page no. 105)

3. Skandh Chakra

(Mentioned in The Third Trimester on page no. 109)

4. Mushtika Bandh

(Mentioned in The Third Trimester on page no. 105)

5. Toe Bending

(Mentioned in The Second Trimester on page no. 88)

6. Ankle Bending
   (Mentioned in The Second Trimester on page no. 89)
7. Ankle Rotation
   (Mentioned in The Second Trimester on page no. 89)
8. Titli Asana
   (Mentioned in The Third Trimester on page no. 109)

Week 3 (till completion of two months from delivery)

With week 2 asana, add following new postures for practice:

1. Chakki Chalanasana
   (Mentioned in The Third Trimester on page no. 103)
2. Namaskarasana
   - Sit in squatting position with the feet flat on the floor about two feet apart.
   - The knees should be wide apart and the elbows placed against the inside of the knees.
   - Bring the hands together in front of the chest in a gesture of prayer.
   - Press the elbows against the insides of the knees.
   - The eyes should remain closed.
   - Inhale and bend the head backwards.
   - Simultaneously, use the elbows to push the knees as wide apart as possible.
   - This is the starting position.
   - Feel the pressure at the back of the neck.
   - Hold this position for three seconds while retaining the breath.
   - Exhale and straighten the arms directly in front of the body.
   - At the same time, push in with the knees, pressing the upper arms inward.
   - The head should be bent forward with the chin pressed against the chest.
   - Tense the muscles of the upper back and shoulders as if someone is pulling the hands forward.
   - Hold this position retaining the breath for 3 seconds.
   - Return to the starting position and bring the palms together in front of the chest, bending the head back.
   - This is one round.

Namaskarasana

Repetition: Practise 5 to 8 rounds.

Breathing: Inhale while bringing the palms together in front of the chest and exhale while extending the arms forward and retain.

Benefits: This asana has a profound effect on the nerves and muscles of the thighs, knees, shoulders, arms and neck. It increases flexibility in the hips.

3. Uttanpadasana

(Mentioned in Pre-Pregnancy on page no. 25)

4. Pad Chakrasana

- Lie down on your back with palms flat on the asana spread on your floor.
- Inhale deep and raise the right leg 10 cm from the ground but keep it straight. Hold the left leg straight on floor.
- Rotate the entire right leg clockwise 10 times in as large a circle as possible.
- The heel should not touch the floor at any time during the rotation.
- Rotate 10 times in the anticlockwise direction.
- Repeat with left leg.
- Do not strain.
- Rest in the base position and do deep abdominal breathing until the respiration becomes normal.

Pad Chakrasana

Benefits: Good for hip joints, obesity, toning of abdominal and spinal muscles

5. Pawanmuktasana

(Mentioned in Pre-Pregnancy on page no. 24)

After two months

It is time to get back to shape. It is a myth to believe that it is impossible to get back the same figure after delivery and more specifically after caesarean section. With yoga and a balanced diet you can look like your previous self even after childbirth.

Take the case of Mrs. Seema Sharma from Saharanpur, who gained so much weight during her second pregnancy that after the birth of the child she began to hate her own look in the mirror. The stretch marks added to her horror. She almost went into depression. However, before it was too late she decided to take up yoga therapy for getting back into shape. She religiously followed her yoga and diet plan for around three months and got back her original shape and with it became her usual cheerful self again.

Lactation

Yoga Therapy

Asanas as stated in obesity and post-pregnancy 3rd week asanas.

Mothers with caesarean section of delivery are advised to start these workouts after completion of 5 months.

Diet during Lactation

Adequate nutrition of the mother during lactation is as important as adequate nutrition during pregnancy. The nutritional link between the mother and the child continues even after birth as for the first few months of life the child solely depends on breast feed and derives all the nutrition from the mother's milk. Researches show that there is no other food equivalent to breast milk for a new born baby. Generally child is breastfed for 6 to 9 months. There are many misconceptions about breast-feeding in the mothers regarding loss of figure, loss of their charm and sagging of the breast etc. Remember, this will never happen to the mothers who breast-feed their child for optimum period.

In fact, breast-feeding has several advantages for the baby as well as for the mother. Physiologically, breast-feeding helps the uterus regain its normal size from the enlargement during pregnancy and reduces the chances of mastitis and breast cancer.

Psychologically, it develops an emotional bonding between the mother and the child and releases stress of the mother she went through after childbirth. Mother forgets all her pains after feeding the child.

As the mother has to nourish a fully developed and rapidly growing infant, she needs extra nutrients to meet the baby's needs in addition to her own requirements. Nutritional needs of the lactating mother are higher than that of the pregnant mother.

Dietary requirements during lactation

Energy requirement

Lactating mothers need additional energy for production of milk, to meet the high BMR during this period and for the conversion of food energy into milk energy. On an average, a lactating woman secretes about 800 to 850 ml milk, the calorific value of which is about 500-600 calories (about 65 calories per 100 ml of milk). So the metabolism involved in producing this amount of milk requires about 200 to 400 calories. Based on an optimal milk output of 850 ml and conversion efficiency of 80%, the additional energy requirement suggested by ICMR during first six months of lactation is 550 kcal/day. If the mother wishes to continue breast-feeding beyond this period then an extra allowance of 400 kcal/day is recommended for the period from 6 to 12 months of lactation. Always remember that the mother who feeds her baby must have adequate storage of energy required during the entire lactating period.

Protein requirement

Protein needs are also increased for the production of milk as the average protein content of breast milk of Indian women is 7.2 gm. An average milk volume of 850 ml during the lactating period increases the protein allowances of the lactating lady from 45 gm/day to 70 gm/day, therefore an increase of 25 gm/day. For proper milk production, adequate amounts of good quality and or complete proteins should be consumed daily.

Mineral requirement

Calcium: The calcium content of breast milk of Indian women is about 30 to 40 mg/100 ml. To meet the additional needs 500 mg of calcium is recommended along with normal requirements of 500 mg. Thus 1 gm of calcium is recommended for a lactating mother.

Iron: Iron requirement during lactation is the sum of the requirement of the mother and that is required to makeup the iron secreted in the breast milk. The concentration of iron in breast milk is about 0.72mg/600 ml. In most of the lactating mothers, menstruation does not take place therefore nearly 1 mg of iron is saved which would otherwise have been lost in the menstrual blood. This amount is sufficient to compensate for the iron secreted in the mother's milk. Thus the total iron requirement is the same as required during pregnancy.

Other minerals: Other mineral requirements are same as that of a pregnant woman.

Vitamin requirement

Vitamin A: A lactating mother needs an ample amount of vitamin A in the diet because milk is a rich source of this vitamin. The quantity of vitamin A in 600 ml of mother's milk is 300 mg and to meet this requirement 300 micrograms of this retinol or 1600 micrograms of carotene is recommended for a lactating mother up to 1 year of lactation.

Vitamin C: The quantity of vitamin C in human milk is 15 to 30 mg. ICMR has recommended an additional intake of 40 mg of this vitamin per day during lactation making it to a total of 80 mg of ascorbic acid per day.

Thiamine: The thiamine content of breast milk is 60 micrograms per 600 ml. Thiamine demand varies according to the demand of energy needs which are increased during lactation. 0.5 mg thiamine per 1000 kcal is recommended for lactating mothers.

Riboflavin: The maximum amount of riboflavin which can be secreted through milk is 30 micrograms/100 ml. This extra amount has to be met through the diet. Therefore, an additional intake of 0.3 mg/day of riboflavin is recommended for lactating mothers.

Folic acid: 25 micrograms of folic acid per day is secreted in the breast milk by the mothers. ICMR has recommended an additional requirement of 150 micrograms of free folate/day.

Fluid requirement: Intake of fluid is increased during lactation. Water and beverages should be consumed in adequate quantity.

Other nutrients: The proper intake of other nutrients is as important as above mentioned nutrients. Their requirements are same as mentioned for a pregnant woman.

(To see the food sources of the above-mentioned nutrients, refer to pregnancy diet section on page no. 72-74)

Special menu plan

MEAL	TIME	MENU		
		Exchange 1	*Exchange 2*	*Exchange 3*
Early Morning	6.30 am	Tea/coffee with cookies of your choice	Tea/coffee with cake rusks	Tea/coffee with biscuits
Breakfast	9.00 am	Idli sambhar with coconut chutney and orange/guava	Aloo methi parantha, curd, butter and apple	Broken wheat (dalia) porridge in milk, besan chilla and banana
Mid-morning	11.30 am	Fresh mix fruit juice and panjiri	Fresh carrot, amla beetroot juice and malai coconut ladoo	Fresh pomegranate, sweet lime, pineapple juice and groundnut or til chikki
Lunch	1.00 pm	Chana dal, brinjal bharta, pineapple sweet raita, chapatti, cucumber, sprouts, tomato salad and suji kheer	Dal makhani, (whole urad dal and kidney beans), stuffed tomato (cheese stuffing), chapatti, rice, cucumber raita, salad of sprouts, and jaggery after meal	Lobia curry, methi gajar aloo vegetable, chapatti, rice, bottle gourd raita, green salad with sprouts and rice kheer

MEAL	TIME	MENU		
		Exchange 1	*Exchange 2*	*Exchange 3*
After lunch	3.30 pm	Til gur ka ladoo	Besan ka ladoo	Kaju barfi
Evening tea	5.15 pm	Banana milkshake, roasted cashew and groundnut along with pistachio and walnuts, vegetable cutlets	Strawberry milkshake, vegetable upma/ idli with tamarind chutney and roasted peanuts	Cashew milk shake, mix vegetable pakoras/ mix fruit chaat/ sweet potato, lotus stem chaat
Dinner	8.15 pm	Clear vegetable soup, moong dal, mix vegetable, chapatti/rice, ice cream or fruit custard.	Spinach tomato soup, bottle gourd curry, cauliflower peas potato vegetable, chapatti/ rice, fruit cream Hot almond milk	Rasam, vegetable sambhar, dum aloo, chapatti/ rice, moong dal halwa
Bedtime	11.00 pm	Hot almond milk		Hot almond milk

Recommended Dietary Allowances

Every individual possesses different nutritional requirements based on age, sex and amount of activity performed. According to Indian Council of Medical Research (ICMR), Recommended Dietary Allowances (RDA) is defined as the intake of nutrients derived from diet which keeps nearly all people in good health. RDA are given for different groups – adults, infants, children, pregnant and lactating women. The nutritional needs also depend upon the amount of work or the type of activities performed by the individual. There is a large variation from individual to individual in occupational activity. ICMR has classified them as light (sedentary worker), moderate (moderate worker) and heavy (heavy worker). Same is applied to the pregnant ladies; every expecting mother has different nutritional requirement depending upon the nature of work they perform in everyday life. Let us have a look at the nutritional needs of pregnant women. This will help you in revising your diet patterns according to your needs.

A. Recommended dietary allowances of various nutrients during pregnancy (ICMR, 1999)

Vitamin A														
Group	Energy	Protein	Fat	Calcium	Iron	Retinol	Beta Carotene	Thiamine	Riboflavin	Niacin	Pyridoxin	Vit. C	Folic acid	Vit. B_{12}
	Kcal/d	*g/d*	*g/d*	*mg/d*	*mg/d*	*ug/d*	*ug/d*	*mg/d*	*mg/d*	*mg/d*	*mg/d*	*mg/d*	*ug/d*	*ug/d*
Sedentary worker	2,175	65	30	1000	38	600	2,400	1.1	1.3	14	2.5	40	400	1.5
Moderate worker	2,525	65	30	1000	38	600	2,400	1.3	1.5	16	2.5	40	400	1.5
Heavy worker	3,225	65	30	1000	38	600	2,400	1.4	1.7	18	2.5	40	400	1.5

B. Recommended dietary allowances of various nutrients during lactation (0 to 6 months) (ICMR, 1999)

Vitamin A														
Group	Energy	Protein	Fat	Calcium	Iron	Retinol	Beta Carotene	Thiamine	Riboflavin	Niacin	Pyridoxin	Vit. C	Folic acid	Vit. B_{12}
Kcal/d	g/d	g/d	mg/d	mg/d	ug/d	ug/d	mg/d	mg/d	mg/d	mg/d	mg/d	ug/d	ug/d	ug/d
Sedentary worker	2,425	75	45	1000	30	950	3800	1.2	1.4	16	2.5	80	150	1.5
Moderate worker	2,775	75	45	1000	30	950	3800	1.4	1.6	18	2.5	40	400	1.5
Heavy worker	3,475	75	45	1000	30	950	3800	1.5	1.8	20	2.5	40	400	1.5

A Lifelong Package for
PERFECT HEALTH
The Complete Guide for Body & Mind
www.vspublishers.com
V&S PUBLISHERS
PERFECT HEALTH
THE COMPLETE GUIDE FOR BODY & MIND
BODY DIET & NUTRITION
PERFECT HEALTH
THE COMPLETE GUIDE FOR BODY & MIND
FITNESS & SLIMMING
PERFECT HEALTH
THE COMPLETE GUIDE FOR BODY & MIND
HEALTH HAZARDS & CURE
PERFECT HEALTH
THE COMPLETE GUIDE FOR BODY & MIND
STRESS & ALTERNATIVE THERAPIES
क्या आप माँ बनने जा रही हैं...?
मातृकला
Ayurveda for All
Effective Ayurvedic self-cure for common and chronic ailments
Symptoms and Causes
Prevention and Treatment
Herbal Therapies & Nature Cure
Nutrition & Diet
FIT & FINE IN BODY & MIND
Healing Power Of MEDITATION
Revised & Updated Edition
YOGASANAS and SADHANA
Road To Health Care
Dr. Seema Kumar
Ladies weight loss Programme
How to have Sound Sleep – the Natural Way
मोटापा
कारण एवं निवारण
न्यू लेडीज़ हेल्थ गाइड
(New Ladies Health Guide)
सफल घरेलू इलाज
योग और भोजन द्वारा रोगों का इलाज
visit our website: www.vspublishers.com

amazon.in/vspublishers

"To sell books is only the beginning of our mission, to build an avid audience of readers who are enriched by these works–that is our ultimate purpose"

V&S PUBLISHERS
VALUE & SUBSTANCE

GOOPU BOOKS® · DELHI · HYDERABAD · THE GEN X SERIES · EXCEL

HOME · EBOOKS · BEST SELLERS · ACADEMIC BOOKS · CHILDREN BOOKS · HINDI · ENGLISH IMPROVEMENT · REGIONAL BOOKS · COMBO PACKS

V&S PUBLISHERS

RAPIDEX COURSES · RELIGION · OLYMPIADS · CHILDREN STORIES · ENGLISH IMPROVEMENT · SELF HELP · DICTIONARIES · SCHOOL BOOKS · CRAFT & HOBBY · HEALTH · ACADEMIC · GENERAL KNOWLEDGE

Bestsellers · Subjects · Olympiads · E-books

Publishers of Olympiads
School Books & General Books

- V&S PUBLISHERS
- EBOOKS
- BEST SELLERS
- ACADEMIC BOOKS
- CHILDREN BOOKS
- HINDI
- ENGLISH IMPROVEMENT
- REGIONAL BOOKS
- COMBO PACKS
- STUDENT DEVELOPMENT
- COMPUTER & IT
- WOMEN ORIENTED
- FAMILY & RELATIONSHIP
- SELF HELP
- HEALTH & FITNESS
- RELIGION & SPIRITUALITY
- LEISURE & LIFESTYLE

Why Should You Read Our Books?

Published by Top Brand
V&S Publishers is a Leading National Level Publisher for Academic & General Books with over 1000 titles published across 50 categories in 10 languages. All books are available as Ebooks on Kindle Worldwide besides being sold as paperbacks through big and small bookstores pan India.

Written by Experts
Each Book is perfectly crafted by Subject Matter Experts & uniquely designed in-house. It offers a rich blended learning & reading experience through simple, quality & informative content. All books are thoroughly edited by experienced editors for grammar, language & factual error.

Assured Production Quality
Production Analysts with decades of experience hand-pick thick, high-quality paper for every book. Each book is machine bound and printed using non-toxic ink at high-end imported printing presses. All books are packaged and singly shrink-wrapped for protection from dust and damage.

On-time Delivery
Each product is exclusively sold by reputed prime sellers & is double-checked for new condition & best in-class packaging standards before despatch. To ensure on-time & rightful delivery, premier courier partners only are chosen for deliveries across all cities.

Buy All Books Online From Our Amazon Brandstore: amazon.in/vspublishers

➤ All V&S Publishers' books are available at best discounts with COD facility on Amazon, Flipkart & Snapdeal.
➤ Search all books by their ISBNs.

➤ अब 'वी एण्ड एस पब्लिशर्स' की सभी लोकप्रिय पुस्तकें COD सुविधा द्वारा Amazon, Flipkart & Snapdeal पर उपलब्ध।
➤ पुस्तक की खरीद के लिए ISBNs नंबर सर्च करें।

Head Office: F-2/16, Ansari Road, Daryaganj, New Delhi-110002, Ph: 011-23240026/27/28 Email: sales@vspublishers.com
Regional Office: 5-1-707/1, Brij Bhawan (Beside Central Bank of India Lane) Bank Street, Koti, Hyderabad-500 095
Ph: 040-24737290 Email: vspublishershyd@gmail.com

V&S OLYMPIAD GUIDE BOOK AND WORKBOOK SERIES (CLASSES 1-10)

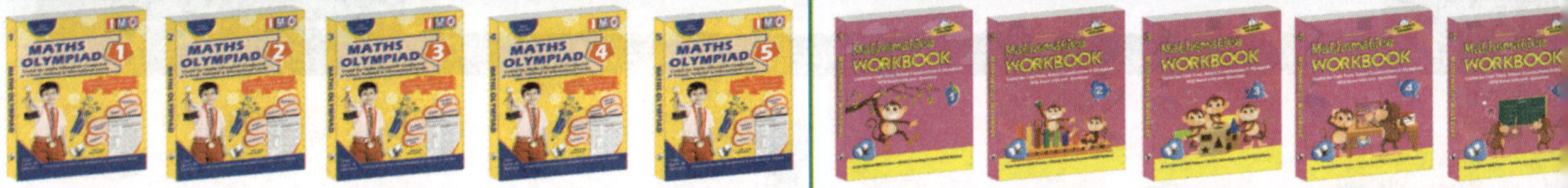

ISBN : 9789357940504 ISBN : 9789357940511 ISBN : 9789357940528 ISBN : 9789357940535 ISBN : 9789357940542 ISBN : 9789357942447 ISBN : 9789357942454 ISBN : 9789357942461 ISBN : 9789357942478 ISBN : 97893579

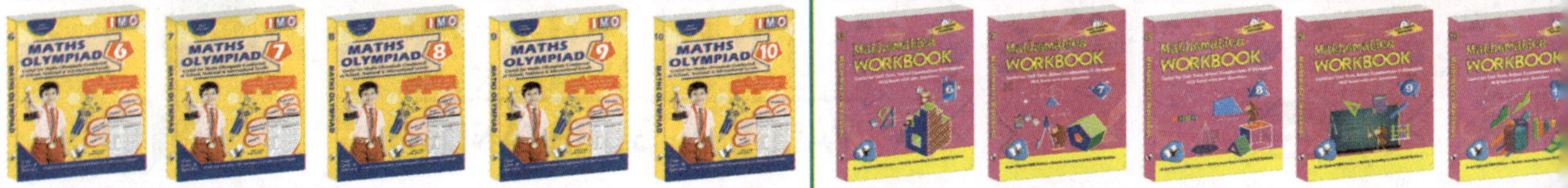

ISBN : 9789357940559 ISBN : 9789357940566 ISBN : 9789357940573 ISBN : 9789357940580 ISBN : 9789357940597 ISBN : 9789357942492 ISBN : 9789357942508 ISBN : 9789357942515 ISBN : 9789357942522 ISBN : 97893579

ISBN : 9789357940405 ISBN : 9789357940412 ISBN : 9789357940429 ISBN : 9789357940436 ISBN : 9789357940443 ISBN : 9789357942546 ISBN : 9789357942553 ISBN : 9789357942560 ISBN : 9789357942577 ISBN : 97893579

ISBN : 9789357940450 ISBN : 9789357940467 ISBN : 9789357940474 ISBN : 9789357940481 ISBN : 9789357940498 ISBN : 9789357942591 ISBN : 9789357942607 ISBN : 9789357942614 ISBN : 9789357942621 ISBN : 97893579

ISBN : 9789357942102 ISBN : 9789357940603 ISBN : 9789357940610 ISBN : 9789357940627 ISBN : 9789357940634 ISBN : 9789357942744 ISBN : 9789357942751 ISBN : 9789357942768 ISBN : 9789357942775 ISBN : 97893579

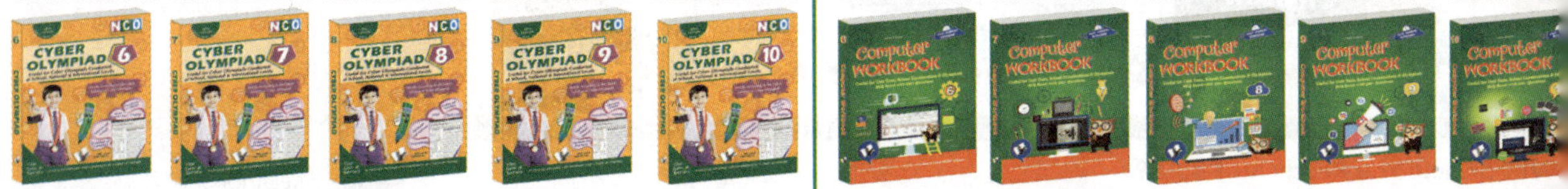

ISBN : 9789357940641 ISBN : 9789357940658 ISBN : 9789357940665 ISBN : 9789357940672 ISBN : 9789357940689 ISBN : 9789357942799 ISBN : 9789357942805 ISBN : 9789357942812 ISBN : 9789357942829 ISBN : 97893579

ISBN : 9789357940696 ISBN : 9789357940702 ISBN : 9789357940719 ISBN : 9789357940726 ISBN : 9789357940733 ISBN : 9789357942645 ISBN : 9789357942652 ISBN : 9789357942669 ISBN : 9789357942676 ISBN : 97893579

ISBN : 9789357940740 ISBN : 9789357940757 ISBN : 9789357940764 ISBN : 9789357940771 ISBN : 9789357940788 ISBN : 9789357942690 ISBN : 9789357942706 ISBN : 9789357942713 ISBN : 9789357942720 ISBN : 97893579

ISBN : 9789357942263 ISBN : 9789357942270 ISBN : 9789357942287 ISBN : 9789357942294 ISBN : 9789357942300 ISBN : 9789357942003 ISBN : 9789357942010 ISBN : 9789357942027 ISBN : 9789357942034 ISBN : 97893579

ISBN : 9789357942317 ISBN : 9789357942324 ISBN : 9789357942331 ISBN : 9789357942348 ISBN : 9789357942355 ISBN : 9789357942058 ISBN : 9789357942065 ISBN : 9789357942072 ISBN : 9789357942089 ISBN : 97893579

CAREER & BUSINESS/SELF-HELP/PERSONALITY DEVELOPMENT/STRESS MANAGEMENT

ISBN : 9789381588789 ISBN : 9789350571637 ISBN : 9789381588512 ISBN : 9789381588963 ISBN : 9789381588598 ISBN : 9789381384039 ISBN : 9788192079622 ISBN : 9789350570753 ISBN : 9789381384396

ISBN : 9789357940115 ISBN : 9789350570968 ISBN : 9789381384527 ISBN : 9789381588666 ISBN : 9789381384541 ISBN : 9789381384107 ISBN : 9789350571187 ISBN : 9789381588574 ISBN : 9789381588277

ISBN : 9789381588222 ISBN : 9789381384213 ISBN : 9789381588772 ISBN : 9789381588949 ISBN : 9789357940108 ISBN : 9789381384152 ISBN : 9789381384145 ISBN : 9789381448564 ISBN : 9789381384473

ISBN : 9789381448595 ISBN : 9789381448670 ISBN : 9789381588253 ISBN : 9789381448755 ISBN : 9789381448649 ISBN : 9789381384480 ISBN : 9789350571309 ISBN : 9789381448632 ISBN : 9789381384893

ISBN : 9789381384091 ISBN : 9789381384176 ISBN : 9789350570265 ISBN : 9789381588727 ISBN : 9789381384411 ISBN : 9789381588246 ISBN : 9789381448687 ISBN : 9789381448786 ISBN : 9789381448533

ISBN : 9789381448526 ISBN : 9789381384206 ISBN : 9788122310689 ISBN : 9789381384503 ISBN : 9789381588505 ISBN : 9789381448717 ISBN : 9788192079646 ISBN : 9789350570203 ISBN : 9789350570272

ISBN : 9789381588741 ISBN : 9789350571170 ISBN : 9789381588215 ISBN : 9789381384763 ISBN : 9789350570296 ISBN : 9789381588284 ISBN : 9789381588543 ISBN : 9789350571880 ISBN : 9789381588765

ISBN : 9789350570579 ISBN : 9789350571927 ISBN : 9789350571545 ISBN : 9789381384114 ISBN : 9789381384435 ISBN : 9789381448779 ISBN : 9789381448991 ISBN : 9789381384510 ISBN : 9789381384169 ISBN : 9789350570623

ISBN : 9789381448908 ISBN : 9789381448915 ISBN : 9789381448922 ISBN : 9789381448939 ISBN : 9789381448946 ISBN : 9789357940795 ISBN : 9789357940801 ISBN : 9789357940818 ISBN : 9789357941303 ISBN : 9789357941853

STUDENT LEARNING/QUIZ/POPULAR SCIENCE/BIOGRAPHIES

ISBN : 9789357941310 | ISBN : 9789357941495 | ISBN : 9789357942430 | ISBN : 9789381384053 | ISBN : 9789381384060 | ISBN : 9789381384121 | ISBN : 9788122310924 | ISBN : 9789381588468 | ISBN : 9789381588604 | ISBN : 9789350570494

ISBN : 9789350570470 | ISBN : 9789350570487 | ISBN : 9789350570500 | ISBN : 9789350570586 | ISBN : 9789350571248 | ISBN : 9789350571248 | ISBN : 9789350571743 | ISBN : 9789381384299 | ISBN : 9789381448052

ISBN : 9789381384305 | ISBN : 9789381384954 | ISBN : 9789381588819 | ISBN : 9789350570371 | ISBN : 9789350570388 | ISBN : 9789350570395 | ISBN : 9789350570401 | ISBN : 9789350570364 | ISBN : 9789381588444

ISBN : 9789381448977 | ISBN : 9789381384459 | ISBN : 9789381384930 | ISBN : 9789350571682 | ISBN : 9789381588864 | ISBN : 9789381588673 | ISBN : 9789350570111 | ISBN : 9789381384312 | ISBN : 9789381588680

ISBN : 9789350570258 | ISBN : 9789350570227 | ISBN : 9789381588499 | ISBN : 9789381588338 | ISBN : 9789381588345 | ISBN : 9789381448656 | ISBN : 9789381384558 | ISBN : 9788192079639 | ISBN : 9789350571019

ISBN : 9789350571026 | ISBN : 9789350571033 | ISBN : 9789350571040 | ISBN : 9789350571057 | ISBN : 9789350570999 | ISBN : 9789350571002 | ISBN : 9789350571064 | ISBN : 9789350571071 | ISBN : 9789350571088

ISBN : 9789350571101 | ISBN : 9789381588321 | ISBN : 9789381588307 | ISBN : 9789381588567 | ISBN : 9789350571163 | ISBN : 9789350570517 | ISBN : 9789381384183 | ISBN : 9789381448625 | ISBN : 9789381384794

ISBN : 9789381384190 | ISBN : 9789381448793 | ISBN : 9789381588192 | ISBN : 9789381588802 | ISBN : 9789381588970 | ISBN : 9789350570777 | ISBN : 9789381448427 | ISBN : 9789350570555 | ISBN : 9789350570548

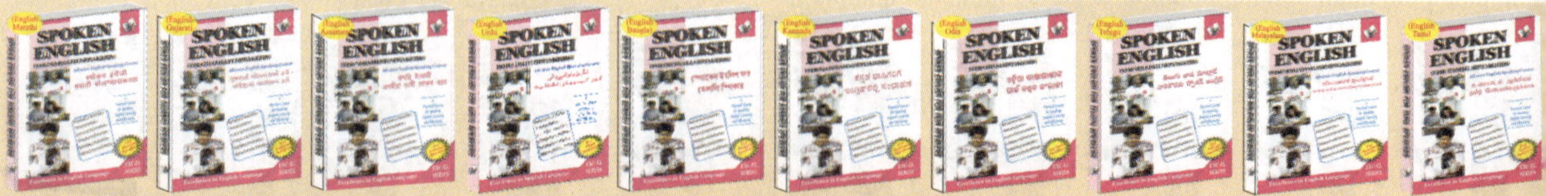

ISBN : 9789357940856 | ISBN : 9789357940849 | ISBN : 9789357941334 | ISBN : 9789357941341 | ISBN : 9789357940153 | ISBN : 9789357940399 | ISBN : 9789357940375 | ISBN : 9789357940382 | ISBN : 9789357941358 | ISBN : 9789357941327

FICTION/FUN & FACT, TALES & STORIES/LEISURE READING

ISBN : 9788192079660 ISBN : 9788192079677 ISBN : 9789381588659 ISBN : 9789381588840 ISBN : 9789381588857 ISBN : 9789381588871 ISBN : 9789381588888 ISBN : 9789381384336 ISBN : 9789381448069

ISBN : 9789381448090 ISBN : 9789381448083 ISBN : 9789381384343 ISBN : 9789381448076 ISBN : 9789381448809 ISBN : 9789381448885 ISBN : 9789350571248 ISBN : 9789350570210 ISBN : 9789381384329

ISBN : 9789381448229 ISBN : 9789381448236 ISBN : 9789350570227 ISBN : 9789381588697 ISBN : 9788192079608 ISBN : 9789350571644 ISBN : 9789381588734 ISBN : 9789350570180 ISBN : 9789381448168

ISBN : 9789381588314 ISBN : 9789381588260 ISBN : 9788192079691 ISBN : 9789381588291 ISBN : 9789381588956 ISBN : 9789350570852 ISBN : 9789350570906 ISBN : 9789350570838 ISBN : 9789350570883

ISBN : 9789350570845 ISBN : 9789350570890 ISBN : 9789350570869 ISBN : 9789350570913 ISBN : 9789350570821 ISBN : 9783950570876 ISBN : 9789350570920 ISBN : 9789350570937

ISBN : 9789381588987 ISBN : 9789350570005 ISBN : 9789350570012 ISBN : 9789350570029 ISBN : 9789381588994 ISBN : 9789350570036 ISBN : 9789350570043 ISBN : 9789350570050 ISBN : 9789381588406 ISBN : 9789350571552

ISBN : 9789381448182 ISBN : 9789381448199 ISBN : 9789381448144 ISBN : 9789381384404 ISBN : 9789381588451 ISBN : 9789381588581 ISBN : 9789381588529 ISBN : 9789381448137 ISBN : 9789381448106 ISBN : 9789381588178

ISBN : 9789381448175 ISBN : 9789381448113 ISBN : 9789381448120 ISBN : 9789381448151 ISBN : 9789381384701 ISBN : 9789381384718 ISBN : 9789381384862 ISBN : 9788192079615 ISBN : 9789381384015 ISBN : 9789381588185

ISBN : 9789350570760 ISBN : 9789350570098 ISBN : 9789350571699 ISBN : 9789350571125 ISBN : 9789357940146 ISBN : 9789357940139 ISBN : 9789350571620 ISBN : 9789350571118 ISBN : 9789350570982 ISBN : 9789350571835

HEALTH & BEAUTY CARE/FAMILY & RELATIONS/LIFESTYLE

ISBN : 9789350570463 ISBN : 9789381588482 ISBN : 9789381448724 ISBN : 9789381448762 ISBN : 9789381448823 ISBN : 9789381384961 ISBN : 9789381384442 ISBN : 9789381448496 ISBN : 9789381588918

ISBN : 9788122307511 ISBN : 9789381448502 ISBN : 9789381384633 ISBN : 9789381448489 ISBN : 9789381384251 ISBN : 9789350570593 ISBN : 9789381384831 ISBN : 9789381384800 ISBN : 9789350570616

ISBN : 9789381384220 ISBN : 9789381384817 ISBN : 9789381384572 ISBN : 9789381448694 ISBN : 9789381384824 ISBN : 9789381384565 ISBN : 9789381384909 ISBN : 9789350570609 ISBN : 9789381448663

ISBN : 9789381448458 ISBN : 9789381384589 ISBN : 9788192079653 ISBN : 9789381384978 ISBN : 9789381448472 ISBN : 9789381448731 ISBN : 9789350571897 ISBN : 9789381448434 ISBN : 9789381448446

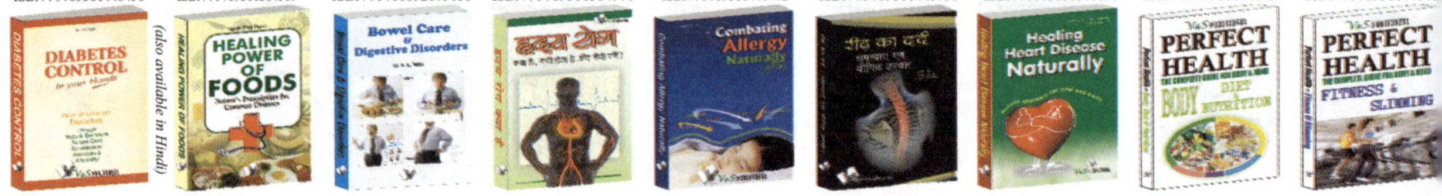

(also available in Hindi)

ISBN : 9789381384244 ISBN : 9789381384237 ISBN : 9789381384626 ISBN : 9789381448519 ISBN : 9789381384619 ISBN : 9789381448892 ISBN : 9789381384602 ISBN : 9789381588369 ISBN : 978938158837

ISBN : 9789381588383 ISBN : 9789381588390 ISBN : 9789381448557 ISBN : 9789381588826 ISBN : 9789381384268 ISBN : 9788122305159 ISBN : 9789381448748 ISBN : 9789381384992 ISBN : 9789381384664

ISBN : 9789381448700 ISBN : 9789381588758 ISBN : 9789381384923 ISBN : 9789350570104 ISBN : 9789381448618 ISBN : 9789381448441 ISBN : 9789381384688 ISBN : 9789381384282 ISBN : 978812230880

ISBN : 9789381448854 ISBN : 9789381384046 ISBN : 9789381384275 ISBN : 9789381384985 ISBN : 9789381448601 ISBN : 9789381448861 ISBN : 9789381384640 ISBN : 9789381384848 ISBN : 9789381384657

ISBN : 9788122310924 ISBN : 9789357940078 ISBN 9789350570357 ISBN : 9789350571200 ISBN : 9789350570340 ISBN : 9789350570944 ISBN : 9789350570951 ISBN : 9789350571309 ISBN : 9789350571828 ISBN : 978935057171

SUBJECT DICTIONARIES/IELTS/ACADEMIC/COMPUTER LEARNING

ISBN : 9789350571576 · ISBN : 9789350571583 · ISBN : 9789350571606 · ISBN : 9789350571590 · ISBN : 9789350571613

ISBN : 9789381588611 · ISBN : 9789381588628 · ISBN : 9789381588642 · ISBN : 9789381588635 · ISBN : 9789381588833 · ISBN : 9789350570326 · ISBN : 9789350570319 · ISBN : 9789350570333

ISBN : 9789350571507 · ISBN : 9789350571491 · ISBN : 9789350571521 · ISBN : 9789350571453

ISBN : 9789350571224 · ISBN : 9789350571231 · ISBN : 9789350571460 · ISBN : 9789350571453 · ISBN : 9789350571484 · ISBN : 9789350571477 · ISBN : 9789350571668 · ISBN : 9789350571538

ISBN : 9789350571392 · ISBN : 9789350571385 · ISBN : 9789350571408 · ISBN : 9789350571330 · ISBN : 9789350571347

ISBN : 9789350571415 · ISBN : 9789350571439 · ISBN : 9789350571422 · ISBN : 9789350571361 · ISBN : 9789350571354 · ISBN : 9789350571378 · ISBN : 9789350571149 · ISBN : 9789350571330

ISBN : 9789350571651 · ISBN : 9789350571286 · ISBN : 9789350571255 · ISBN : 9789350571262 · ISBN : 9789350571293 · ISBN : 9789350571279 · ISBN : 9789350571569 · ISBN : 9789357940368 · ISBN : 9789357941934

ISBN : 9789350571705 · ISBN : 9789350570241 · ISBN : 9789350570234 · ISBN : 9789350571965 · ISBN : 9789357941365 · ISBN : 9789357941549 · ISBN : 9789357941556 · ISBN : 9789357941563 · ISBN : 9789357941570

ISBN : 9789357941501 · ISBN : 9789357941518 · ISBN : 9789357941525 · ISBN : 9789357941532 · ISBN : 9789357941747 · ISBN : 9789357941716 · ISBN : 9789357941709 · ISBN : 9789357941723

ISBN : 9789357941730 · ISBN : 9789350571693 · ISBN : 9789357941655 · ISBN : 9789357941662 · ISBN : 9789357941679 · ISBN : 9789357941686 · ISBN : 9789350570173 · ISBN : 9789381588895

ISBN : 9789350570142 · ISBN : 9789381588536 · ISBN : 9789350570159 · ISBN : 9789350570128 · ISBN : 9789350571316 · ISBN : 9789350571989 · ISBN : 9789350570135 · ISBN : 9789350570166

ISBN : 9789357942232

ISBN : 9789357942379

ISBN : 9789357942256

ISBN : 9789357942386

ISBN : 9789357942249

ISBN : 9789357942393

ISBN : 9789357942225

ISBN : 9789357942362

ISBN : 9789357940054 · ISBN : 9789357940016 · ISBN : 9789357940023 · ISBN : 9789357940085 · ISBN : 9789357940825 · ISBN : 9789357940092 · ISBN : 9789357940009 · ISBN : 9789357940030 · ISBN : 9789357940061

ASTROLOGY/PALMISTRY/VAASTU/HYPNOTISM/RELIGION & SPIRITUALITY

ISBN : 9789381588925 ISBN : 9789381588710 ISBN : 9789381448540 ISBN : 9789381448045 ISBN : 9789381384350 ISBN : 9789381384367 ISBN : 9789381384077 ISBN : 9789357940832 ISBN : 9789381384534

ISBN : 9789381384374 ISBN : 9789350571194 ISBN : 9789381384466 ISBN : 9789381448021 ISBN : 9789381448014 ISBN : 9789381588796 ISBN : 9789381588796 ISBN : 9789381384084 ISBN : 9789381448212

ISBN : 9789381384756 ISBN : 9789381384879 ISBN : 9788122309973 ISBN : 9788122310849 ISBN : 9789381384497 ISBN : 9789381384886 ISBN : 9789381384497 ISBN : 9789381448878 ISBN : 9789381384725

NEW ARRIVALS

ISBN : 9789357941471 ISBN : 9789357941457 ISBN : 9789357941419 ISBN : 9789357941433 ISBN : 9789357941464 ISBN : 9789357941402 ISBN : 9789357941396 ISBN : 9789357941389 ISBN : 9789357941372 ISBN : 9789357941488

ISBN : 9789357941440 ISBN : 9789350571842 ISBN : 9789350571859 ISBN : 9789357942843 ISBN : 9789357941938 ISBN : 9789350571958 ISBN : 9789350571941 ISBN : 9789350571132 ISBN : 9789350571767 ISBN : 9789350571774

ISBN : 9789350571750 ISBN : 9789357941426 ISBN : 9789357942171 ISBN : 9789350571903 ISBN : 9789350571910 ISBN : 9789357940207 ISBN : 9789357940214 ISBN : 9789357940221 ISBN : 9789350571972 ISBN : 9789357940177

ISBN : 9789357940184 ISBN : 9789357940191 ISBN : 9789381384770 ISBN : 9789357942850 ISBN : 9789357941983 ISBN : 9789357941990 ISBN : 9789357940313 ISBN : 9789357940320 ISBN : 9789357941976 ISBN : 9789357941969

ISBN : 9789357940269 ISBN : 9789357940306 ISBN : 9789357940238 ISBN : 9789357940276 ISBN : 9789357940245 ISBN : 9789357940283 ISBN : 9789357940252 ISBN : 9789357940290 ISBN : 9789357941952 ISBN : 9789350571873 ISBN : 9789357941945 ISBN : 9789357941966

ISBN : 9789357940047 ISBN : 9789350571811 ISBN : 9789350571804 ISBN : 9789381384138 ISBN : 9789381384121 ISBN : 9789357940870 ISBN : 9789350571798 ISBN : 9789357940863 ISBN : 9789357942409